W9-ADG-397

Leatherwork
A Step-by-Step Guide

Mary and E. A. Manning

HAMLYN
London · New York · Sydney · Toronto

TT
290
M35

Published by
The Hamlyn Publishing Group Ltd
London · New York · Sydney · Toronto
Astronaut House, Feltham, Middlesex, England

© Copyright The Hamlyn Publishing Group Limited 1974

ISBN 0 600 38099 8

Printed in England by Cox and Wyman Limited, Fakenham

Contents

Introduction

Leather has had a universal appeal from time immemorial. When we see the richness of this wonderfully versatile material and realise the thousand and one uses to which it can be put, it is not difficult for us to appreciate its immense popularity.

Modern manufacturing and finishing techniques have led to the development of a great variety of leathers suitable for clothing. And, as a result, fashion designers now give this material a prominent place in *haute couture*, in addition to its continuing use in the making of accessories.

Added to its versatility and durability, leather has yet another valuable quality which has helped to establish its popularity. This is its 'workability'. Given the correct type of leather, the right tools for the task in hand and simple, straightforward instructions, it is possible for anyone to make useful and attractive leather articles.

All of the articles shown in this book have been designed and made with you, the beginner, in mind. We hope that you will see how easy it would be to copy these designs and how, as your own talent for creative leatherwork develops, you can go on to more ambitious projects.

We hope that, as we work together in this step-by-step guide, you will gain not only in experience but in a fuller appreciation of the beauty of this material. And, of course, the book will help you to save money too: your new skill will enable you to make accessories at a fraction of the retail cost, as well as gifts for your family and friends.

Leatherwork provides you with an unrivalled opportunity to develop your artistic skills, and to enjoy the sense of achievement to be gained through creative work. We hope that by this time you are eager to start working, so we will go on, straight away, in the first chapter, to tell you how to begin and the tools you need for the task.

1 First steps

You will already be familiar with the texture of leather – its feel, its appearance and the different kinds you will have seen used for numerous purposes. Here is an introduction to the various types from which you can make a choice when you want to make a particular article. Like other materials, leather can be bought in numerous qualities and, naturally, the rarer skins are the most expensive.

In a later chapter, we deal with soft leathers and suedes as used in making clothing. Here we will describe leather mainly in terms of accessories and craft work.

Basil comes from the sheep. This leather is home-produced and therefore less expensive than other types. It comes in a wide variety of finishes, many of them realistic imitations of more expensive skins, and it is an easy leather to work on, either by hand or using a household sewing machine.

Hide is a tougher and heavier type of leather, which comes from cattle, cows, bulls, oxen and even horses. A thick and hard-wearing material, this is used for suitcases, shoes and heavier accessories.

Splits, a term which is self-explanatory, are made by dividing hides. When stained and machine-stamped with patterns which imitate natural expensive skins, such as crocodile or pigskin, these are most attractive leathers.

Calf is almost entirely a home product. Prized for its softness and workability, this is an ideal leather for decorative modelling techniques, but it is quite expensive compared with basil. However, once you have gained in experience, you will find this leather rewarding in the making of good-looking and high-quality articles.

Morocco is a fine and deservedly popular leather made from goatskin. The name comes from the special processes used in tanning. This is a most attractive material for fine leather work, although it is one of the more expensive types.

Skivers are leathers produced from split sheepskin. These are thin, flexible materials suitable for lining purposes.

Suede is not one type of leather but a special finish which can be applied to the fleshy side of skins from different animals. The heavier varieties, which come from cowhide, are used in the manufacture of shoes. Lighter types, some of which are made from cowhide, sheepskin, calf, goatskin, pigskin and so on, are available in a wide range of colours. Many of these are suitable for accessories and clothing.

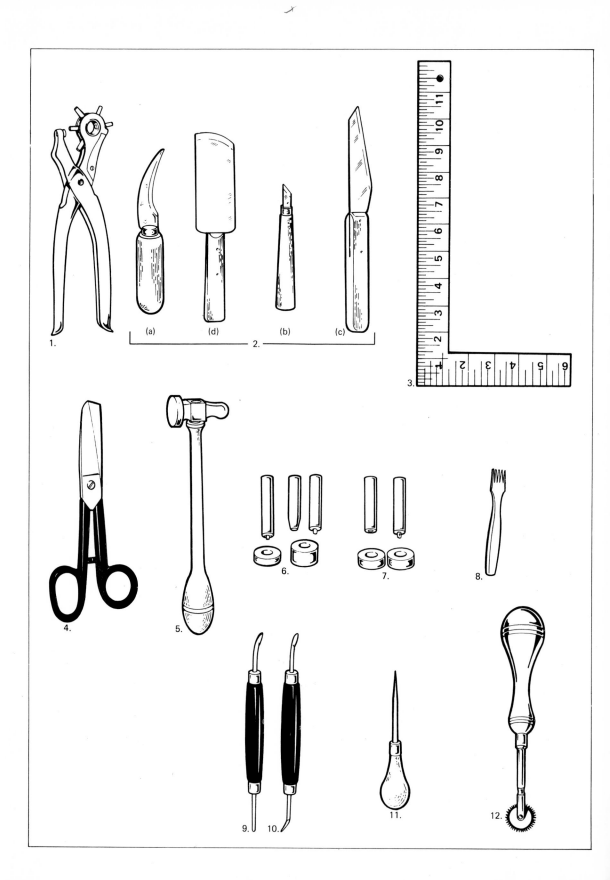

1.

(a)   (d)   (b)   (c)

2.

3.

4.

5.

6.

7.

8.

9.   10.

11.

12.

TOOLS FOR THE TASK

Tools for leatherwork have two great attractions: they are simple and relatively inexpensive. Furthermore, the skill needed to use them is quickly and easily acquired. And, although as a beginner you may not need to possess all of them at first, it is more satisfactory from your own viewpoint if you can learn about each one and practise using them all from the start.

The first thing you need is a good working surface. The ideal would be a large glass or metal plate which you can lay on your table for tasks like cutting or modelling. Do remember that you are likely to damage the wood if you use an unprotected table.

Here are the tools shown in our diagram:

1 Leather punch with revolving head which gives six sizes of punched hole
2 (a), (b) and (c) are knives used for various cutting purposes. (d) is a skiving knife, used for trimming the underside of leather
3 A steel ruler or set-square, essential for accuracy in measuring and cutting
4 Leather shears
5 Leatherwork hammer, needed for numerous tasks
6 Tools for fixing eyelets
7 Tools for fixing press-studs
8 Stitch spacer, an essential guide for hand sewing
9,10 Tools for line marking and modelling
11 Awl for making holes in thick leather
12 Stitch marker which has rotating wheel

WE ARE READY TO BEGIN

Having discussed the types of leather available and the tools you will need for the course, let's now decide where to begin. This first experience should be an encouraging and enjoyable one in using both tools and leather. And the best way to begin is to make something simple and straightforward, yet worthwhile.

Simple handbag

We have decided to start with a simple but attractive handbag, which consists only of four pieces. If you follow the instructions carefully, and check and re-check each step as you go along, you should manage this task easily. You can, of course, also refer to the chapters which follow, for guidance. The accompanying diagrams show how your patterns should be made, and the picture shows how the finished bag should look.

The materials required

1 skin of basil or hide split, for bag; 1 skin of skiver leather, for lining; $\frac{1}{8}$yd of hessian or sailcloth, for stiffening; 4 D-rings; 4 tubular rivets; 10yd of thonging; leather adhesive (a rubber-based type, such as Copydex); simple clasp fastening.

If you look at the drawing you will see that the main part of the bag (the body and base) is made from one piece of leather, and that the essential steps in making the bag consist of fitting in a gusset on each side, attaching handles and completing the top closure.

Making the pattern

To make your pattern, you will need a sheet of brown paper, or squared pattern paper (1in to each square), of the sort sold in haberdashery departments, large enough for the diagrams to be redrawn actual size on it. You will also need a pencil and long ruler or set-square.

If you are using plain paper, start by drawing a rectangle, 21in by 8in, as shown, for the outline of the main section. You will see that the measurement from the top of the bag to the base is 8in on each side, and that the base is 5in across. Mark these points on your outline. The shaping of the top narrows by 1in on each side, to a depth of $1\frac{1}{2}$in. Mark these points at each end of the bag also, and draw in guidelines on the pattern, as shown, to complete.

Mark in details on the pattern such as handle placement lines and the centre point for the clasp fastener at this stage, too. The points marked for attachment of the handles are shown in the diagram, and are 3in from the top edge and $1\frac{1}{4}$in from the outer edge.

If you use squared pattern paper throughout, you will find this a great help when drawing lines and taking measurements, especially if it is marked in 1in squares.

Having drawn the outline of your main pattern section, you are now ready to draw the other pattern pieces by following the diagrams. The gusset pattern should measure 6in by 4in, with rounded corners at one end. The pattern for the top stiffening should be made so that it fits the top of the bag exactly, following the measurements given. The pattern for the handle straps is 17in long and $1\frac{1}{2}$in wide, although of course this can be shortened or lengthened as you wish.

Make a quick check to see that all your measurements are correct. Then cut out your pattern pieces carefully. Now, for extra reassurance, it is best to cut out the main parts of the bag (excluding the handles) in paper. Pin these together carefully, so that you can get a clear idea

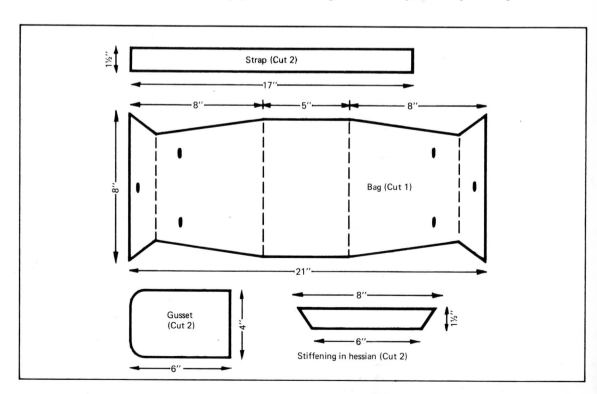

of how the finished handbag should look. Should you find that the pieces do not fit together well or that the structure does not look right, measure your pattern again to check that all measurements are correct.

When you are satisfied that your bag will look right, the next step is to make a working pattern in thin cardboard. This important step should always be followed throughout. A strong card pattern of this sort is much easier to use when marking leather, and it can be put away for use afterwards. Use carbon tracing paper to trace the pattern details on to the cardboard and then cut the cardboard out exactly to the shape required. When storing patterns for future use, mark each piece for identification purposes and store in a large envelope.

Cutting out the bag in leather is the next step and you must be certain that everything you have already done is correct! Take your time about deciding how to place your pattern pieces on the leather for cutting out, as this is another important decision.

Unlike cloth fabrics which you buy by the yard, leather is uneven in shape and it tends to be uneven in weight and texture also. So, even though you have been careful to select a skin which is as free of blemishes as possible, there may still be markings or uneven patches.

As the body of your bag is the part which will be most in view, see that the main pattern piece is arranged so as to have unblemished leather on the back and front of the bag. Make sure also that you will be able to cut the other pieces out satisfactorily from the remainder of the skin, moving the pattern pieces round to see how they fit.

Finally, use a pencil to mark all the pattern outlines on the leather. Mark in any details such as handle placements at this stage, too. Having done that, lay your pattern pieces aside, as you won't need to use them when cutting out the bag.

To cut the leather, you will need a metal ruler or set-square, a sharp, pointed knife and sharp shears. With the leather on a hard surface such as a glass or metal plate, as explained earlier, place the ruler so that its edge is set firmly along the line to be cut. Using one hand to press down on the ruler and hold it in place, draw the edge of the knife firmly against the edge of the ruler and through the leather. It may take several strokes of the knife to complete the cut. Then move the ruler into place for the next cut.

Because cutting is such an important part of leatherwork, and one in which practice is necessary, take time to familiarise yourself with the combined use of knife and ruler by making cuts on waste scraps of leather.

Proceed to cut along all the straight lines of one section, leaving curved edges until last. The easiest way to cut curved edges is by using shears, but you must be sure that the cuts are clean and straight. This means that you will need a sharp pair of shears and a steady hand.

While we are dealing with the subject of cutting implements, it is worthwhile stressing that many used for leather are particularly sharp, so do always keep them out of the reach of children, and be careful when using them yourself.

In this chapter, we have made a start with leatherwork. You have been introduced to pattern making and leather cutting, and you have the sections of a simple bag ready for the next step, making up. This seems a good point at which to take a rest, so leave your work aside for a brief spell and move on to Chapter 2. There you will be able to study carefully some of the next steps in leatherwork, before proceeding to make up your bag.

2 How to join leather

You will see from the sketch that the handbag begun in the previous chapter has no visible hand- or machine-stitching. Instead, the pieces are joined together by thonging. This is the simplest and easiest method to use when you are dealing with a thick material such as leather.

THONGING

The traditional material used for thonging is a thin strip of lacing cut from leather. Like many other products, this is also available in plastic. Leather thonging has many advantages over the artificial variety. It is a natural match for the material on which it is being used and, if it is cut from the same skin, then the blend is perfect. However, it requires more skill and effort to use, mainly because it lacks the firmness of the synthetic type. Another problem is that the cut edges have to be stained, a task that may prove tedious for the beginner.

To cut leather thonging *see Fig. 1*

This shows how a continuous thong can be cut from a circular piece of leather. Your aim should be to cut a thong ⅛ in thick, as this looks neat and will be strong enough for your task. The length of the thong will depend on the size of your circle, which, in turn, will depend on the amount of material available. Obviously, you need a circle which is large enough to give a useful length of lacing.

We shall, of course, be returning to the handbag begun in Chapter 1, presently, which still has to be lined and assembled! Meanwhile, we will show the techniques used in making up the bag, for these are included in the instructions for punching and thonging which follow in this chapter.

Further on in the book we have a chapter dealing with linings and fastenings. These are important also in the making of your bag, and you should study the instructions given carefully, especially with regard to lining. But for the present, we will assume that your linings are already attached to the bag sections, and that you are ready to join them together by thonging.

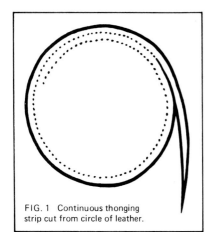

FIG. 1 Continuous thonging strip cut from circle of leather.

Punching holes

The first step in preparation for thonging is to punch holes in the leather. These should be quite small, evenly spaced and they should be made *after* the lining has been attached. Another important point is that the holes punched in one section should match exactly those in the section to which it is to be joined: otherwise, the sections will be unevenly joined together.

The tools you can use for punching are the leather punch, (1) and the stitch marker, (12), in the illustration which shows leather tools. You will also need a ruler and a finely pointed pencil. Before starting to make holes in the leather, it is essential that their positions should be marked evenly on the entire area to be punched.

Using your ruler and a very light pencil touch, draw a faint line $\frac{1}{8}$in from the outer edge of the leather. Then, still using the ruler and pencil, mark dots along the line at $\frac{1}{4}$in intervals: starting at a corner, the first dot should be $\frac{1}{8}$in from each of the two edges at the corner. By beginning at a corner, you should be able to make any slight adjustments necessary in spacing the dots to ensure that dots at other corners are evenly spaced too. Ideally, such adjustments should occur at the base of the bag, where they won't be seen.

Instead of using a pencil for marking, you can use the stitch marker mentioned earlier. If you hold the ruler firmly with its edge $\frac{1}{8}$in from the edge of the leather, you can run the wheel of the marker close to the edge. This method will produce a row of dots, and if you punch every second dot, you will get an even row of holes. However, you may prefer to use a pencil for marking until you have become more experienced, as this makes for easier organisation of corner spacings.

You are now ready to begin using the leather punch. Turn the head of the punch until the No. 1 cutting edge is in position for cutting. Resting the main part of the leather on the table and using a piece of cardboard as a backing, centre the punch arm over the mark on the leather and press firmly. When you feel the punch cutting, give your wrist a slight twist and the tiny piece of leather will come out cleanly.

As with other operations, it is worthwhile practising this on waste scraps before you begin. Apart from the need to make holes evenly, you must beware of the risk of punching too close to the edge; since incorrectly punched holes obviously cannot be removed, this is an essential precaution.

Matching gusset markings
Having punched holes round the edges of the (lined) main section of your bag, the time has come to mark corresponding points on the gussets (also lined). Do be careful, for, if the holes punched in the gussets do not match those in the area of the bag to which they are to be joined, the entire structure will be wrongly shaped.

The best way to make sure that the gusset and bag sides will fit together correctly is to mark the centre of the bag's base at the edges on each side. The base of your bag is 5in from back to front, so your centre marking will be $2\frac{1}{2}$in from the lower fold. If you mark the centre of the curved end of the gusset to correspond with this, your gusset markings can be made evenly from the centre outward on each side.

The handle of the bag is made by folding the strip in two lengthwise and thonging the edges neatly together. In this case, too, it is essential that the punch holes should be a perfect match on each side of the strip. Follow the same procedure to prepare the two handle strips for thonging.

The art of thonging
At first glance, thonging seems such a simple procedure that it is difficult to see how one could go far wrong with it. Yet mistakes can easily be made. If you study the illustrations and instructions which follow, you will see the problems that can arise and how easily most of them can be avoided. And we also show you how you can make your work more interesting, by varying your thonging technique.
Fig. 2 shows how you can tie edges to be joined together temporarily, when preparing for thonging.
Fig. 3 Here we solve the problem of concealing the end of your thonging

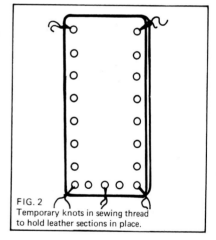

FIG. 2
Temporary knots in sewing thread to hold leather sections in place.

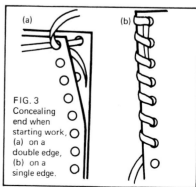

FIG. 3
Concealing end when starting work, (a) on a double edge, (b) on a single edge.

when you begin to join two pieces together. Leave the end long enough so that it can be held securely and concealed between thonging stitches on the inside and leather on the outside. In this way it will not show.

Fig. 4 What to do with the finishing end of a thonging strip – you don't want it to rip out and it mustn't show. If the point is easily accessible, run the thonging end underneath the previous three or four stitches on the wrong side, and apply a drop of rubber-based adhesive to hold it in place. If it is not accessible, then apply a little rubber-based adhesive to the remaining length of thonging and press it against the leather on the wrong side of the bag. Be especially careful not to cut ends of thonging too short when completing a task.

Getting round corners

Fig. 5 shows you how to cope with corners. (a) represents an ugly pointed corner with thonging unattractively arranged; in (b) the same corner has been trimmed to a curve and a double stitch gives a nicer finish. (c) shows a rounded corner evenly thonged. Points should always be trimmed off at corners, as a curved effect looks best.

Fitting gussets

A gusset is a shaped piece of material designed to give a bag (or a garment, for that matter) shapeliness and spaciousness. In *Fig. 6* we show five different types of gusset used in the making of bags of all descriptions. At first glance, these may look alike, but if you look closely you will see why some of them are more easy to manage than others when it comes to fitting them.

6a is the type of gusset used in the bag which you started in Chapter 1.

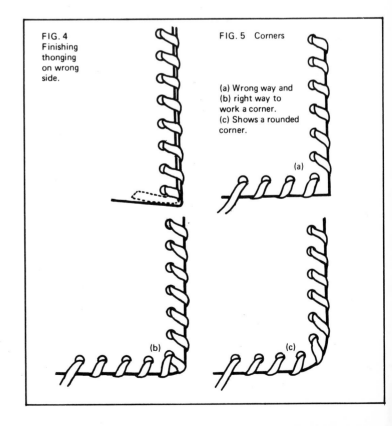

FIG. 4
Finishing
thonging
on wrong
side.

FIG. 5 Corners

(a) Wrong way and
(b) right way to
work a corner.
(c) Shows a rounded
corner.

(a)

(b)

(c)

This has a rounded shape at the lower end, and can be fitted into a bag cut all in one piece, or into one in which the base is separate from the sides.

6b is another version of the same type of gusset. The difference is that here the lower ends are square, and only the points at the corners have been trimmed off for neatness.

6c shows a V-shaped gusset fitted into an envelope-style bag. This is narrow at the lower end, where it fits neatly into the fold of the bag, and it widens out at the upper end. As you can see, it is pressed to fold inwards when the bag is closed.

6d is a more difficult type of gusset to fit, simply because it runs in one long strip to form sides and base, and has to be joined to two separate back and front pieces.

6e is another version of *6d*, the difference here being that the gusset is folded in two lengthwise (with right sides facing one another) to give it an inward fold when it is attached to the bag.

Usually the gusset is made from the same material as the main part of the bag. Occasionally, however, you may find it easier to make it from a lighter leather in the same shade: in making folding gussets as shown in Figs. 6c and 6e, for example. But it is worth remembering that if you do use a softer leather for such purposes, this must be straight and firm enough to give an even fit.

Fitting gussets is one of the most important steps in bag making. If the gussets do not match and are not correctly fitted, the entire bag will be pulled out of shape. In such an event there is nothing for it but to rip out the incorrectly fitted gusset – something to be avoided because of the risk of marking and fraying the leather in the area of the punch holes.

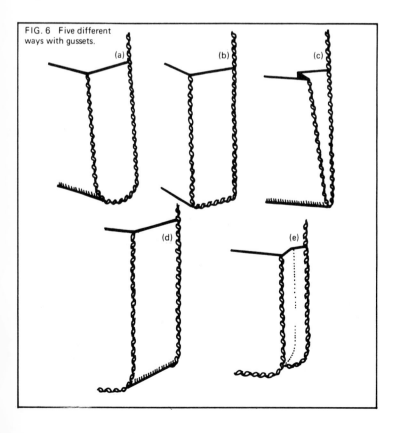

FIG. 6 Five different ways with gussets.

(a) (b) (c) (d) (e)

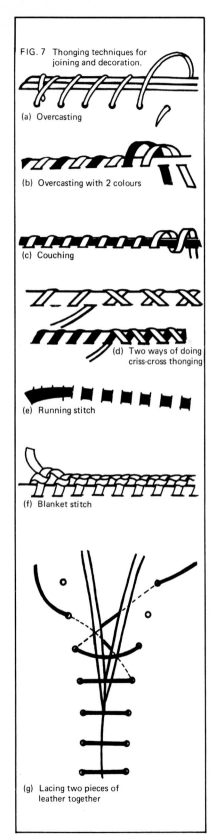

FIG. 7 Thonging techniques for joining and decoration.

(a) Overcasting

(b) Overcasting with 2 colours

(c) Couching

(d) Two ways of doing criss-cross thonging

(e) Running stitch

(f) Blanket stitch

(g) Lacing two pieces of leather together

When we explained how you should punch the holes in your bag and make matching holes in the gusset, we stressed the need to mark the centre line of the bag's lower fold and the centre line at the lower end of the gusset. It is this even matching at both sides of the bag which is the determining factor in getting the whole structure to sit right and look right.

Having made this important centre marking on the wrong side of both gusset and bag, measure both carefully to match the gusset to the front and back edges of the bag. These points must also match precisely, to ensure that each gusset fits well, and that the two gussets are level when the bag is completed. In *Fig. 2* we show you how to use sewing thread to tie each gusset in place temporarily before you start to thong the pieces together.

Use the same marking system when assembling bags such as those shown in Figs. 6a, 6b and 6c. And this is, of course, the method to use when making up the bag you have already cut out and punched.

The gusset shown in Fig. 6d is somewhat more difficult to fit. However there is no need to be put off by this thought, you may find this a very useful type of gusset to use when you are short of material and cannot cut out the main part of a bag all in one piece.

In the case of the gussets shown in Figs. 6d and 6e, there is a larger and longer area to be matched on both sides, but once you have marked all the pieces correctly, there is no reason why they shouldn't match.

Start by punching the back and front sections of the bag, and mark the centre lower edge of each panel on the wrong side. Using a ruler for guidance, mark the centre of the gusset on each side, where it is to match with the centre line markings on the front and back panels. Then, with equal care, mark the gusset on each side where it is to match with the lower corners of the bag.

To get the gusset to match exactly, lay the edge of the panel to which it is to fit along the edge of the gusset, and mark the gusset for punching through the holes already made in the front and back panels. Finally, before starting to thong the sections together, tie back and front panels to gusset at the following points, following the method shown in Fig. 2: centre lines, corner and top edges. In this way you will know whether or not your gusset will be a perfect fit *before* you start to join the pieces together.

Different ways with thonging

Fig. 7 shows how variations can be introduced to make thonging not only a useful technique for joining two pieces of leather together, but also a decorative effect. The most widely-used method, and the one which we have described and shown so far, is the simple overcasting method. However, as you gain experience and master early problems, you will want to be more adventurous.

With regard to essential details, thonging techniques follow ordinary sewing techniques very closely. You will appreciate this when you look at the names given to them:

Fig. 7a shows *overcasting*, the method on which all the others are based, and the simplest one for the beginner.

Fig. 7b A more sophisticated version – *two-colour overcasting*. The technique is precisely the same in each case.

Fig. 7c shows *couching*. Here again we have overcasting, with a difference. An extra strip of thonging is incorporated to give the effect of an edge-trim.

Fig. 7d Two ways of producing a *cross-stitch*. First a line of overcasting is made. Then a second line is inserted to go in the opposite direction, using the same or a contrasting shade of thonging.

Fig. 7e The familiar *running stitch*. This is often seen as a trim or as a joining technique on thick leathers.

Fig. 7f shows *blanket stitch* or *point de ganse*. As in the case of ordinary sewing, this involves taking the end of the thonging through the loop formed as each stitch is being made. The result is a plaited effect along the edge. Because of its softness and pliability, leather thonging is best for this work.

Fig. 7g shows how you can get an interesting effect when joining leather for belts and other items by *lacing* them together. Starting on the wrong side with a firm stitch, you simply lace two ends of thonging through evenly matched holes in shoe-lace fashion.

Slits instead of punch holes

For variety and novelty, you may use slits instead of holes to take the thonging. For this method, you will need to use the pronged spacer and punch numbered 8 in the illustration showing leather tools.

To use this tool, you will need to have your leather on a flat, firm surface and the line to be punched should be marked lightly. Holding the punch in one hand with the prongs on the line, use a hammer to tap the prongs through the leather. For perfect evenness, when making successive cuts, place an end prong in the last slit made until the work is finished. If you plan to do much of this type of work, it would be a good idea to add a small pair of single-slit pliers to your stock of implements. This is a tool you will find very useful when dealing with corners.

You will also need to use a special blunt-pointed needle for this type of thonging. It should have a large eye through which the thonging can be threaded. You may find that you already have a tape needle or bodkin which might be suitable for this task.

It is sensible to practise each new technique on waste scraps of leather. Doing this can save you time and frustration, not to mention the possible waste involved in making mistakes on expensive materials.

MACHINE AND HAND SEWING

(See also Chapter 6, which deals with sewing in relation to the soft leathers and suedes used for clothing).

You will find your sewing machine an invaluable aid in your leather-work. In fact, there are certain tasks for which machine stitching is most suitable. These include sewing pockets to linings and stitching in zip fasteners, where these are being used. However, special care is necessary in working with a material which is of a very different nature to cloth fabric.

Many sewing machine manufacturers provide instructions for sewing leather and leather fabrics, so see if guidelines are supplied in the instruction book which came with your machine. Here are a few simple rules which apply to most sewing machines:

1 Experiment on scraps of leather of the same weight as the piece you are going to use, until your stitch length and tension are correct.
2 Use a leather needle in size 14–16. You can buy packets of these from your sewing machine stockist. It is possible, however, to use an ordinary needle in the same size – preferably a new one.
3 Adjust the stitch length to between 8 and 10 stitches per inch.
4 Check tension and pressure. The tension should be fairly loose but balanced evenly. A light pressure is usually best.

5 Use a suitable sewing thread, such as mercerised cotton.

6 Avoid having to rip out stitches as far as possible, by stitching carefully.

7 Take care not to stretch the leather as you stitch. Seams should be $\frac{3}{8}$in wide. Use sticky tape or clips to hold the edges together before stitching.

8 Do not backstitch to begin or end seams. Instead, tie thread ends together to secure the stitching.

9 Pre-shrunk tape may be used to reinforce seams at weak points. Where seam allowances should lie flat, use a rubber-based adhesive to hold them in position. Where appropriate, flat seams may be top-stitched on right side.

10 To eliminate bulk, wedges should be cut out of seam allowances on curved edges, as shown in *Fig. 1*.

HAND SEWING

Hand sewing is a more highly regarded, but slower and more difficult process. Nevertheless, there are many tasks in leatherwork which are best done or finished by hand; if you can afford the time and patience necessary for this kind of work, your reward will be worth waiting for. It is only fair to say, however, that the classical hand-stitched leather articles one sees in the shops are the products of highly-skilled and dedicated craftsmen. And because their task isn't an easy one, or one which can be completed hastily, such articles are very highly priced.

For hand stitching you will need a suitable leather needle and a thimble. Use mercerised cotton or linen thread, and you will find that stitching is easier if you use candle wax or beeswax to wax the thread. Another tool you will need is a stitch spacer. For light hand work, this should mark ten or twelve stitches to the inch. For coarser and heavier leather, you will need fewer stitches per inch.

Stitch markings should be evenly placed $\frac{1}{8}$in from the cut edge, as shown in *Fig. 2b*. This diagram also shows how you can use two needles and two lengths of thread, each making a continuous running stitch to give added strength to the seam. However, the most commonly-used stitch is the single running stitch seen in *Fig. 2a*.

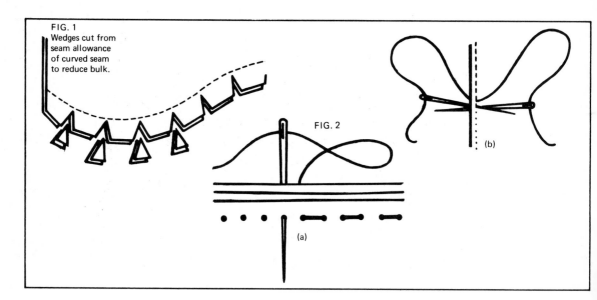

FIG. 1
Wedges cut from seam allowance of curved seam to reduce bulk.

FIG. 2

(a)

(b)

Instructions for the patchwork document case are on page 36, and those for the simple writing case are on page 41.

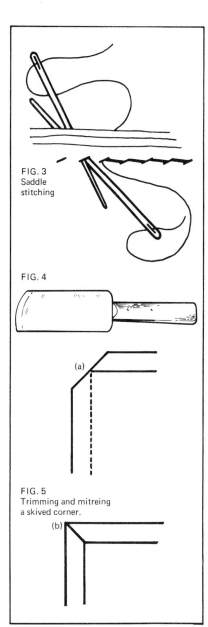

FIG. 3
Saddle
stitching

FIG. 4

(a)

FIG. 5
Trimming and mitreing
a skived corner.

(b)

For soft leathers, you can use a gloving needle, which is specially sharpened for ease in puncturing the material. When sewing heavier leathers, you will need to use the awl to puncture a hole at each stitch marking before a stitch can be made. For this type of work the best needle to use is a saddler's needle.

Whichever hand sewing method you use, it is important to make sure that stitching threads are drawn up firmly to give the correct tension. They should not be too tight, as it can spoil the appearance of the leather. To start work, you can use a knot on the end of the thread, so long as this is well concealed when the work is completed. In addition to the knot, you can make a few back stitches at the beginning of the row. Rows of stitching should be finished off with back-stitching, and then the remaining thread can be concealed inside the joining on the wrong side, or between leather and lining, if a lining is being used.

Saddle stitching

The classical saddler's stitch is shown in *Fig. 3*. Used to join sections of heavier leather, this employs the two-needle technique. First the stitches are marked, then an awl is used to punch the stitch holes. Finally, the two needles are inserted into the same hole, so that they go in opposite directions. The thread should be waxed.

Skiving for neat joinings

Skiving is the term used to describe the trimming of leather edges in preparation for seaming, to reduce bulk. This involves a careful paring of the edges on the underside of the leather, and is necessary when the leather is thick. The implement used for this purpose is a skiving knife, which has a bevelled blade. You will see from *Fig. 4* that this looks rather like a carpenter's chisel and it is used in much the same way.

The leather to be trimmed should be marked $\frac{3}{16}$in from the raw edge on the under-side, by making a faint line in pencil. Then, holding the leather firm and right side down, trim the edge by pushing the knife away from you, with the bevelled edge of the blade to the leather. It is important to have a very firm glass or metal base underneath the leather for this work.

As a result of skiving the edges you will have a thinner layer of leather all round. You can now turn this skived edge in over the leather (or leather and lining) to form a hem on the wrong side. Use a little rubber adhesive to hold the turned-in edge neatly in place for stitching. And do remember to make an allowance for leather thus treated, for it will be $\frac{3}{16}$in smaller than the original measurements. If the article being skived has square corners, trim off the corners, as shown in Fig. 5a. Then fold in the edges at each corner to get a mitred effect, as shown in 5b.

Finally, before starting to sew, place a piece of cardboard over the turned-in area of leather and use a hammer to tap the cardboard gently. This flattens and neatens the doubled part.

Staining edges

Leather dyes should be used very lightly to stain any edges that are going to show in the finished article. This will be necessary in thonged or stitched work where there is a stuck-on lining cut flush with the edge. Be careful not to stain the body of the work. This risk is less likely if a light stain is used very sparingly.

3 Fastenings and fittings

Although there are many leatherwork fittings you can make, you will find factory-made fasteners and other fittings in plentiful supply. These help to give a professional finish to your work and, where tools are required to enable you to attach them, these are inexpensive and simple to use (see illustration of leatherwork tools in Chapter 1).

In the illustration, right, we show you some of the large variety of metal fittings available for use with leather. These can be purchased in handicraft and leather shops and in the haberdashery departments of some large stores. The sketches include the following:

Fig. 1 D-rings in sizes $\frac{1}{2}$in, $\frac{5}{8}$in, $\frac{3}{4}$in and 1in, in a nickel or brass finish, can be used to attach handles, as clasps in belts and in any position where a metal link is required. When attaching a D-ring to a bag, a small strap wide enough to fit the flat part of the ring is used to enclose it. This strap is then doubled and stitched to the bag.

Fig. 2 shows a key case fitting. Many similar fittings can be obtained to enable you to make a variety of articles.

Fig. 3 shows a selection of press-studs. These are available in various sizes and colours, and a simple tool is used to attach them to the leather. Another item in this class is the eyelet which comes in various sizes and colours.

Figs. 4, 5 show tubular and split rivets, items which can be used for many purposes where you wish to avoid stitching.

Fig. 6 shows a base dome, useful on the base of a heavier bag or case.

Fig. 7 Fastenings are important. They make for an attractive finish and, of course, they must be serviceable as well as good-looking. The turn button fastener set shown here is very easy to fit. You can obtain this in different shapes.

Fig. 8 Attaché case fittings are very easy to fit.

Fig. 9 Clapette edge-closure fastens securely.

Fig. 10 Simple craft closures of the kind you can make yourself are very popular, although they do not usually make such a secure fastening as the bought variety. However, you could combine this kind with a press-stud.

Fig. 11 The correct way to insert a zip fastener, with the zip closed.

Zip fasteners

No type of fastener surpasses the zip in popularity or efficiency, especially for leatherwork. However, fitting a zip, even into a cloth fabric setting, can lead to problems, so it is worthwhile taking steps to avoid these.

In leatherwork, the zip should be fitted into the area for which it is intended *before* the remainder of the work is completed. The opening into which the zip is to fit must be cut carefully. If the leather is thick, it will help if you skive the edge, as explained in the last chapter.

Having decided on the length of zip you are going to use and where it is to be situated, start by measuring and using a ruler to mark the

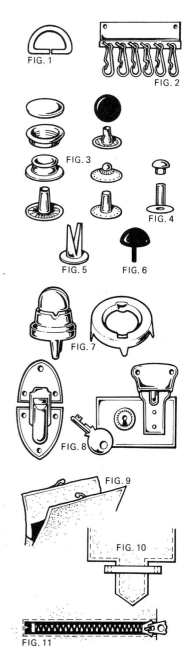

FIG. 1
FIG. 2
FIG. 3
FIG. 4
FIG. 5
FIG. 6
FIG. 7
FIG. 8
FIG. 9
FIG. 10
FIG. 11

This child's suit in soft leather could be made by adapting an ordinary dressmaking pattern, using our instructions.

*The shopping bag and knitting holdall can be made by following the
instructions on pages 36 and 37.*

area to be cut out. The opening should be long enough to accommodate the length of the zip plus $\frac{1}{8}$in for ease in insertion. Then it should be wide enough along the entire length to accommodate the widest part of the zip, the moveable head, but narrow enough to allow the tape to be caught by the stitches on each side. An extra $\frac{1}{8}$in added to the width of the head should be sufficient to take care of these problems.

Use your ruler and knife to cut the zip opening. Then on the under-side of the leather, mark a line $\frac{3}{16}$in from the cut edge all round. Using the skiving knife as described in Chapter 2, trim the under-surface to reduce the thickness. The next step is to place the zip fastener face-downward on the wrong side of the leather, in the position required. Use a light application of rubber adhesive to stick the tape to the wrong side of the leather and strips of sticky tape as a temporary expedient to secure the zip tape all round.

You are now ready to stitch the zip in place. You can do this by hand, of course, but machine stitching is stronger and faster. Work with the zip to the right of the machine's presser foot. If there is difficulty in getting the leather to move under the presser foot (as can happen when the leather is thick or has a shiny finish), place a layer of tissue paper between the foot and the leather.. If you stitch through this, it can easily be torn away when the zip insertion has been completed. For extra strength where a zip will be subjected to frequent use, a second row of stitching $\frac{1}{4}$in outside the first can be added.

Handles and straps

Handles and straps are an essential part of most bags. Generally, these are of two types. The simplest form is just a straight strip of leather cut from a suitable area of the skin. This can be a narrow band with a backing of lining or fabric stuck on, and stitching for reinforcement. Or it can be wide enough to be doubled in two along its length and then stitched. Yet another variation, which is suitable for light leathers, is to cut the strap three times the desired finished width. When this strap is folded in three and stitched, the result is a hardwearing and neatly-finished band. Any of these straps would be suitable for a shoulder bag, and if a buckle is used to join two straps, the length can be adjusted as required.

For shorter straps and handles for shopping bags, where the wear is likely to be considerable, corded or piped strips are often used. In *Fig. 1* we show *(a)* the shaping of the handle with cord in position, ready to have the edges joined by thonging. A corded handle can also be made by machine. In this case, the handle must be wide enough for the double edge to be held under the presser foot of the machine. The surplus is trimmed off evenly afterwards. Naturally, the handle finish will depend on whether the rest of the bag is stitched or thonged.

Next, we come to the matter of attaching handles and straps to the bags. This can be done by stitching or thonging the ends to the outside of the bag, as shown in Fig. *1b* where, as you can see, the ends are shaped attractively for a well-finished appearance. Or the handles can be attached to D-rings which, in turn, are attached to the bag by a double band of leather, as shown in *Fig. 1c*.

Usually, the second method described is best. It allows for more flexibility in the movement of the handles and there is less wear and tear on the leather of the bag. This is the method recommended for the first bag that you are making – the one discussed in Chapter 1.

Handles should be attached to the bag before it is lined and stitched up. The positions for attaching either the handles themselves or the

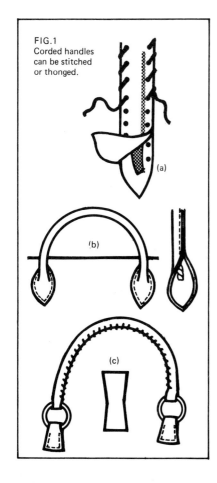

FIG.1
Corded handles can be stitched or thonged.

(a)

(b)

(c)

D-ring straps should be clearly marked when the bag is being cut out. Another way of attaching the D-ring straps is to make small slits in the bag and insert the ends of the straps so that they remain on the wrong side of the bag, where they are kept in place by stitching and decorative rivets. *Fig. 2* shows handles attached in this way.

Lining and pockets

You can make a lining from a fine natural leather such as a skiver intended for the purpose, or you can use a fabric lining such as duck or sailcloth. If you are using a cloth fabric, a firm one such as one of the above-mentioned will be easy to handle, as well as giving body to more flexible kinds of leather.

Linings and pockets are dependent upon each other, and they must both be completed before the bag is assembled. An inner pocket stitched to the lining material can be of any size, provided that it is well clear of the edges to be stitched. Mark the position of the pocket on the right side of the lining. Machine-stitch a hem on the top of the pocket and stitch it to the lining panel, being careful to make stitching secure at upper corners.

An outside pocket is slightly more complicated. Again, this must be stitched in place before the bag is assembled but after the position of handles has been decided. Ideally, an outside pocket should follow the outer line of the bag. It should be placed so as not to interfere with the handle attachment and, for security, a zip fastener or flap with press-stud can be incorporated.

Fig. 3 shows two different ways of attaching outside pockets. In *3a*, a pocket is cut from the same leather as the bag. A zip fastener is then inserted in the pocket (following the directions given earlier in this chapter), so that it is placed about 2in from the top edge of the pocket and about 1in from each side. The pocket is then stitched to the bag panel.

In *3b*, the pocket has a flap with a press-stud closure. In this case, pocket and flap should be cut out and checked carefully to see that they fit together well. The position of the pocket is marked on the bag and the flap is stitched in place first (with the point upwards, insert two rows of stitching across the lower end). Finally, the pocket is stitched in place so that the upper edge is matched to the flap end. Pockets can be lined or unlined – this depends to a great extent on the thickness of the leather.

Lining

Whatever type of lining is used, the best way to attach it is to stick it to the wrong side of the leather. This sort of lining should be attached after pockets and handles have been fixed in place. The easiest way to line a bag is to stick all the pieces, panels, gussets etc, to the skin used for lining, smooth all creases out carefully and then cut the lining evenly around the edges of each section. If necessary, the cut edges can then be stained before the work is punched, ready for thonging.

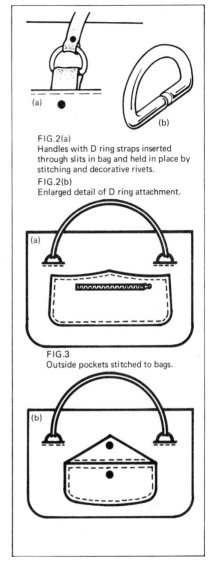

(a)

(b)

FIG.2(a)
Handles with D ring straps inserted through slits in bag and held in place by stitching and decorative rivets.

FIG.2(b)
Enlarged detail of D ring attachment.

(a)

FIG.3
Outside pockets stitched to bags.

(b)

This smoothly-shaped waistcoat, gently flared from the waist, could be sewn using several pieces of matching leather or suede.

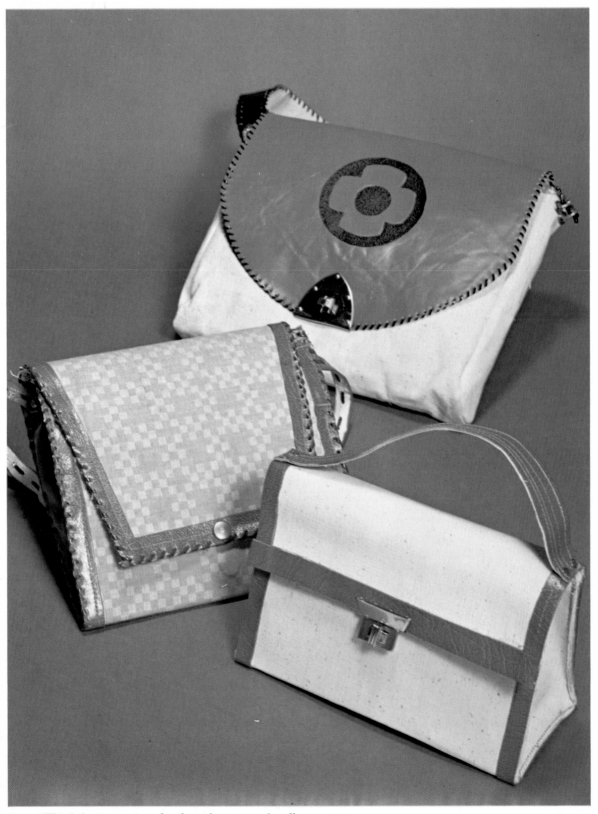

You will find the instructions for these three smart handbags on pages 38, 39, and 43.

4 Decorative work

Because of its softness and flexibility, leather is a material which lends itself admirably to artistic effects. The very soft varieties such as suede are ideal for the technique known as appliqué: this involves stitching on decorative motifs in different shades to a garment or accessory. Then, for the heavier types, such as calf and hide, tooling and modelling techniques can be used to produce ornamental work of great beauty. Both of these methods involve marking the leather with special implements, so that it retains the desired impression. Finally, there are staining and dyeing processes which can be used either on their own or in combination with other decorations.

Tooling

As you will soon discover, the surface of leathers like calf and hide can be marked very easily. While this may be a worry when you are trying to avoid spoiling the material, it is a quality which can be turned to good purpose when a simple decoration is required.

The simplest decoration to produce is one which relies for its effect on lines. These may be curved, straight or a combination of both: a combination of geometrical shapes can look very attractive. You can use your own artistic flair to design an original pattern for tooling, or you may like to copy something you have seen in a book or magazine. Embroidery transfers are another source of inspiration: in this case, you may wish to use only one or two details from the transfer, and, of course, you must not attempt to use heat to transfer the design to the leather, as you would in the case of a cloth fabric.

Whatever kind of design you use, and no matter how simple it is, you should make a pattern on paper first. If, for instance, you want to decorate a bag or a blotter cover, work with a paper pattern of the article. Mark this carefully to make sure that the design will be accurately and evenly placed in relation to the shape of the article. Then fill in all the details you wish to include.

Only when you are perfectly satisfied that every detail is correct on paper, should you transfer your design to the leather. The stage at which tooling or modelling should be done is before any joinings have been made. This leaves you with a flat piece of leather, which you can place, face upward, on a hard, smooth working surface.

To transfer patterned designs to the leather, start by fixing the paper pattern firmly to the leather, so that it won't move and spoil your design. A good way to do this is to use sticky tape to attach the edges of the pattern to the back of the leather panel all around. You can also use paper clips for extra security, but you must be careful to see that these don't mark the edges of the leather.

Let us assume that your design is a simple pattern of lines going in various directions. Using the straight end of the modelling tool shown in our illustration of tools, and a ruler, draw the lines of the design on the paper pattern. You will need to use sufficient pressure to make sure that the lines appear on the surface of the leather. In the same way, you can transfer the other details of your design to the leather.

When you have done this, remove the pattern paper and work over all the lines of your design again, using the straight end of the modeller, to make sure that the leather surface has a clear impression of every detail.

The next step is to damp the surface of the leather, since this will help you to get a deep, lasting impression. Even if you are decorating only a small area of the panel, you should dampen it all over, to avoid staining. Using a sponge, moisten the entire surface well, but not so that the leather is soaking wet. Allow the moisture to penetrate the surface before starting work. Afterwards, as you work over the design, you can sponge over any areas which tend to dry out prematurely.

As with all other processes, it is a good idea to practise each step on a waste scrap of leather. In this way, you will know exactly how the effect will look when you mark the leather in a particular way. Your aim is not to tear the surface but to depress each line you make as deeply as possible without cutting it, so the way you hold the lining tool is important. Hold it as you would hold a pencil, to draw and redraw the same line repeatedly, while applying pressure.

For straight lines, use a ruler as a guide. For circles and curves, look around for some household article which is the right size to use as a guide: an egg cup or the base of a small bottle or tin, for example.

A small punch with a design stamped on it can be used very effectively to fill in background areas. This is an extremely simple method, since all you have to do is to hold the punch vertically on the part to be decorated, strike the upper end with a hammer, and repeat the process until the desired area has been stamped.

Fig. 1 shows a simple tooled motif. The lines have been tooled by using the tools shown in *Fig. 2*. The dotted areas have been stamped by using one of the punch stamps illustrated in *Fig. 3*.

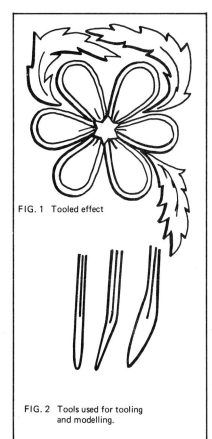

FIG. 1 Tooled effect

FIG. 2 Tools used for tooling and modelling.

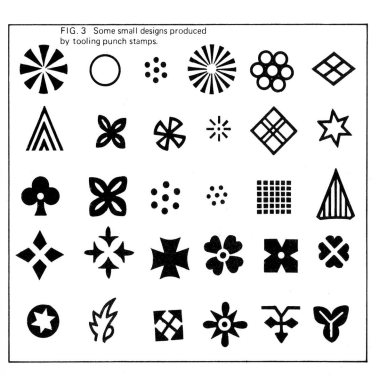

FIG. 3 Some small designs produced by tooling punch stamps.

We tell you how to make the delightful dog on page 79: stitch the little girl's pinafore out of leather, too.

Six bags in all shapes and sizes for you to choose. Instructions are on pages 40, 44, 45, 46, 48 and 54.

You can get a deeper and darker impression of the tooled design on the leather by heating the implements used. All that is needed is to hold the metal point of the modeller or punch in the flame of a gas jet for a moment or two, being careful not to get your fingers burnt. Test the heat on damp leather scraps. It should make a slight but not loud hissing noise, because if it is too hot it will scorch the leather. Wipe the heated point on a clean, dry cloth before using it, to make sure that it is clean.

Modelling

Although it is an extension of leather tooling, modelling gives much wider scope, and, of course, it requires greater skill and patience to accomplish.

The technique involves transferring designs to leather in the same way as for tooling. The essential difference is that with modelling, the background of the design is pressed downwards all around, so that the design is shown in relief. To transfer the details of your design to the leather, follow the directions given for tooling. The leather should also be damped in the same way.

Use the broadest tool shown in *Fig. 2* to press down the background to the design you have drawn. Practise using this tool on spare scraps and you will see how pressure can be exerted on the base, edges and point to give clear lines and work into corners, as well as on flat areas.

This work requires time and patience, if you are to obtain the best results. However, if you are modelling a smallish design on a large area, there is no need to press down the entire background. To obtain good effects you need only model the leather in the area immediately surrounding it.

Fig. 4 shows a handbag with a modelled decoration on the flap. You can use a great variety of motifs for this work. Some of the most popular traditional types include leaves, flower and geometrical patterns. Nowadays, when colourful designs in the Greek, Celtic and African traditions are so popular, the possible choice is immense.

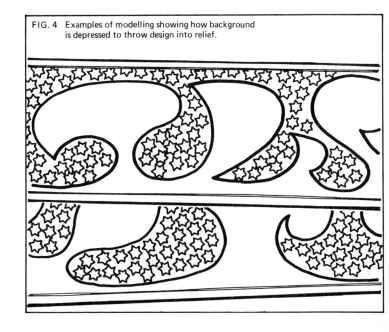

FIG. 4 Examples of modelling showing how background is depressed to throw design into relief.

Staining

Tooling and modelling both look very well on plain leather, when they depend for their total effect on line and workmanship. However, if you want to introduce more interest into your design, a wide range of leather stain is available.

Stains specially designed for leather are available in powders, which are soluble either with boiling water or methylated spirit. Because it dries more quickly than the water stain, the spirit stain is generally more popular.

Having selected the shade you wish to use, it is important to remember to dissolve the powder thoroughly in order to avoid patchy work, and that you mix sufficient stain for your task: these are rules which apply to any work which involves the mixing of paint or dye, of course, so you can appreciate their importance when dealing with work as delicate as staining leather.

Having prepared your stain, test it on a scrap of the leather to be used. Allow the stain to dry, so that you can judge the strength of the colour obtained. Usually it is better to apply two or three coats of weaker colour than one coat of very strong stain. It is a good plan not to overdo the staining, especially when it is being applied to a carefully modelled area. Too many colours can result in the effects of modelling and tooling being lost. Another tip is not to stain the entire area of the panel. If you leave outer border areas clear, the attractive quality of the natural leather can make its contribution to the total effect.

Before preparing the work and applying the stain, study the instructions provided by the manufacturer. The area to be stained should be moistened (but not damped) by swabbing it over with water or methylated spirit. If a large area is to be stained, a pad of wadding or cotton wool can be used. For smaller areas, it is best to use a soft brush and apply the stain in a circular motion.

When the stain has dried completely, a thin application of white wax polish may be used to shine the panel.

Dyeing and painting

You can obtain wonderfully colourful effects by using the latest Dylon leather dyes and paints. The range includes paint-on colours and dyes suitable for different purposes, and the manufacturers give clear instructions with regard to the types of colouring suitable for leather and how the task of dyeing or painting should be carried out.

Appliqué

As the name implies, this technique involves cutting out scraps of material and applying them as a decoration to a larger area. You will know how this method can be used to produce attractive designs on clothing and felt backgrounds. It can be employed equally well when working with suede and soft leathers. It is one of the easiest methods of decorating, and since it is one which depends for its effect on colourful scraps of material, it is a good way of using up suitable leftovers.

You couldn't use traditional embroidery stitches to apply leather appliqué, even if you wished, so it's just as well that other methods are available. The easiest method is to draw geometrical or floral design patterns in paper, use these paper patterns to cut out the leather, and stick the leather motif to the main material. A rubber-based adhesive will hold the pieces in place firmly, and if there is no strain in the area you don't need any stitching. However, in most cases, it is best to

A fashionable suede jacket like this will stay smart for ever.

stitch the design in place: to do this, use a wide zigzag stitch and machine round the edges of the motif. *Fig. 6* shows zigzag machine stitch for appliqué outline. *Pattern* on page 45 is for bag with tooled, modelled or painted design on the front flap. *See pattern* on page 43 for a bag with an appliqué design on the flap.

To make these bags, follow instructions given elsewhere in the book for lining, gussets, thonging and handles.

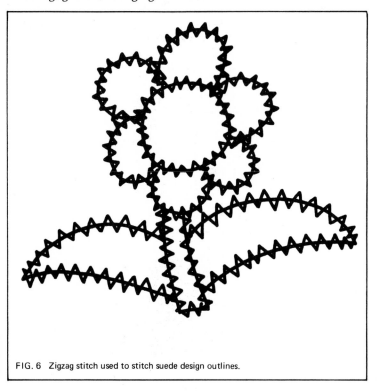

FIG. 6 Zigzag stitch used to stitch suede design outlines.

5 Items to make

In this chapter we deal entirely with items, large and small, that you can make for yourself. The first thing, of course, is to complete the handbag begun in Chapter 1, so this is the first item on the list.

FINISHING YOUR FIRST BAG
By the end of Chapter 1, you had cut out the pieces for your bag and the small pieces of hessian for stiffening the back and front top areas. The two chapters to which you should now refer are Chapter 3, dealing with linings, handles and fastenings, and Chapter 2, which shows how to carry out punching and thonging techniques and how to fit gussets. Here is a step-by-step guide to the work you have to do:
1 Trim the hessian stiffenings by cutting off $\frac{1}{8}$in round all the edges. Using adhesive, stick the stiffenings to the wrong side of each end, so it is $\frac{1}{8}$in from the edge all around.
2 Make and attach handles, as shown in Chapter 3.
3 Stick the body of the bag and the two gussets firmly to the wrong side of the lining, as explained in Chapter 3. Cut the lining so it is flush with the leather to which it is attached.
4 Mark and punch holes in gussets and bag as shown in Chapter 2. Use thonging to assemble bag, as shown.
5 Following instructions supplied with fitting, attach Clapette fastener to centre of top of bag.

Compact needle case

Here we have used a remnant left over from the first bag.

Requirements
Leather – piece cut to measure 12in by $3\frac{1}{2}$in; lining (skiver), 12in by $3\frac{1}{2}$in; smaller (unlined) leather piece, $3\frac{1}{2}$in by 3in; 3in square of flannelette or woollen material. *Fittings* – 1 $\frac{1}{4}$in press-stud; approximately 1yd thonging; rubber-based adhesive, such as Copydex.

To make the case
Cut out two leather pieces (one large and one small), as shown in diagram.

Trim one end of the larger piece to a curve, as shown, and mark position of press-stud at centre and punch one hole. Fold the piece of leather in three with the curved edge outwards and overlapping, so that it reaches the lower fold. Carefully mark the position of the second half of the press-stud by inserting the tip of a pencil through the hole already made in the flap. Fix the under-part of the fastener in place.

Next, the lining: trim one end to match the curved end of the outer

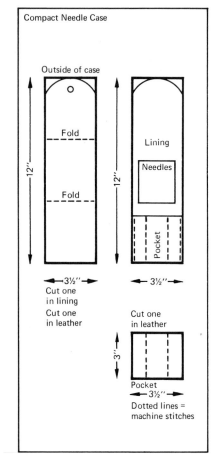

Compact Needle Case

Outside of case

12″

Fold

Fold

3½″
Cut one in lining
Cut one in leather

Lining

Needles

Pocket

12″

3½″
Cut one in leather

Pocket

3″

3½″
Dotted lines = machine stitches

leather. On the other end, stitch the pocket as shown in the lining diagram. Now stick the lining evenly and smoothly to the outer leather. Use the cutting punch to extend the hole already made in the outer part of the flap through the lining, and fix the upper part of the press-stud in place.

To complete, punch-thong the edge all round and stick the fabric square (which will hold needles) to the lining as shown.

Belt pouch

A useful accessory and perhaps the nearest that the modern young man gets to wearing a handbag!

Requirements
Leather – Piece of hide from which to cut the following: 1 main piece, 16in by 4in; 2 gussets, each 5in by 1½in; 2 straps, each 4in by 1in. *Fittings* – one ½in press-stud and 2yd of thonging.

To make pouch
Cut pieces, as shown in the diagram. Shape one end of the large piece, as shown, and punch hole for press-stud. Fold piece in three along lines indicated and, using pencil, mark for under press-stud through hole already punched in flap. Fix both studs in place.

Stitch two belt straps to back of pouch, allowing slight slackness for fitting over belt.

Fit gussets as shown in Chapter 2, and thong gussets in place. To complete, thong neatly round raw edge of flap, top of gussets and front of pouch. This pouch does not require a lining.

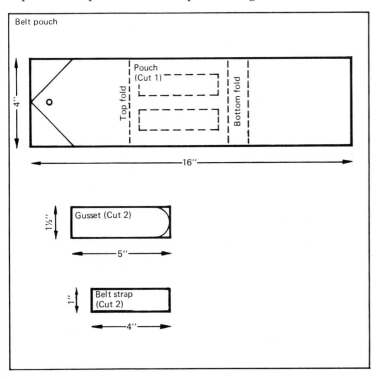

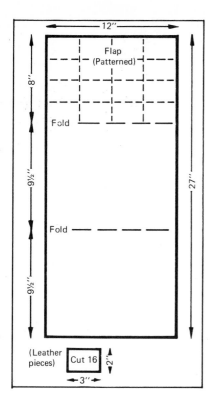

School document case

This document case, which is shaped like an envelope, was made from leftover pieces of leather and lining material.

Requirements

Leather – from leftover leather, cut 16 pieces in various colours, each measuring 3in by 2in. However, the number and size of pieces are optional, so long as they fit neatly into the area designed to form the flap. This measures 12in by 8in, in the case made. *Sailcloth* – 1 piece measuring 27in by 12in. Two or 3 pieces joined together could be used. *Lining material* – we used one length of coat lining which measured 27in by 12in, to fit the sailcloth length. Satin bias binding – 1 card. *Fitting* – 1 turn button handbag fastener.

To make the case

With wrong sides together, stitch lining to sailcloth around all edges, and use bias binding to neaten edges. With material opened out flat and lining downwards, use rubber adhesive to stick pieces of leather neatly to flap end of case, as shown in diagram. With leather upwards, use large zigzag to stitch all the pieces of leather in place, using three rows of stitching vertically, and three horizontally. Mark centre of flap and fit top part of fastener. Fold material along lines indicated and fit underpart of fastener. Machine-stitch sides of case, to make joining on each side.

A Dorothy bag

The leather chosen for this bag is a dark brown split with a light-coloured leather lining.

Requirements

Leather – about 2sq ft of leather and the same amount for lining. The skins must be large enough to enable you to cut one piece 18in by 10in from each, and two circular bases, each 6in across. *Fittings* – six $\frac{1}{4}$in brass eyelets; three $\frac{1}{4}$in split rivets (bifurcated domes); 5yd brown thonging; 1yd cord, in matching or contrasting shade; Copydex adhesive. This bag can be enlarged to suit individual taste, in which case the measurements must be increased in proportion.

To make the bag

First measure and mark your leather. Then, using steel ruler and knife, start by cutting out the large 18in by 10in section, in brown leather. Use a set-square to check that the angles are correct.

Next, on the reverse side of the leather, draw a circle 6in across, as shown in diagram. Use your shears to cut out the circle carefully.

Now cut out the lining. Here again, you need two pieces. Cut the main lining piece so that it is $\frac{3}{4}$in shorter than its leather counterpart (18in by $9\frac{1}{4}$in). This difference is necessary to reduce bulk when the outer leather is folded over at the top of the bag.

Mark six evenly spaced points for the eyelets, $1\frac{1}{2}$in from the top line all around. Start by marking a point $1\frac{1}{2}$in from each end and allow 3in between each of the other points. Now, using a suitable punch,

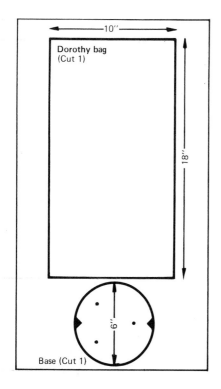

cut the six holes for the eyelets. Most haberdashers can supply a complete punch and eyelet kit.

The next step is to attach the lining pieces to the main fabric. Use Copydex or a similar rubber-based adhesive to stick both sections together, remembering to leave a $\frac{3}{4}$in margin free at the top on the large outer piece, for turning in.

Finish punching the eyelet holes through the lining, and insert the eyelets according to instructions supplied with the eyelet kit.

Turn the $\frac{3}{4}$in allowance at the top in over the lining, and use adhesive to paste this down firmly. You are now ready to punch the main part of the bag for thonging, so mark and punch round the edges on three sides, omitting the top edge, as shown in the thonging instructions earlier.

Now we return to the circular base. Insert the three split domes to form a triangular pattern in the outer material. Next, paste on the lining. Matching the holes already punched round the lower edge of the main piece, mark and punch all round the edge of the base. You are now ready to thong the base to the top and to join the edges of the bag together. Insert cord through eyelets and tie ends to complete bag.

Knitting bag

Requirements

Leather – Cut from a soft, flexible skin of basil the following pieces: 1 large piece, 14in by 12in – mark and trim at corners as shown in diagram; 1 gusset, 20in by 4in; 2 handles, each 20in by 2in; 2 small squares to form end tabs, each 2$\frac{1}{2}$in by 2$\frac{1}{2}$in. *Fittings* – 1 12in zip fastener.

To make bag

Cut out patterns and leather pieces, as shown. Following directions given for zip insertion in Chapter 3, cut opening in gusset, centring it so that it is placed 4in from each end, and stitch in zip fastener. Shape each of the small square pieces at one end. Stitch one at each end of the gusset, so that the straight end is 1in below the end of the zip fastener.

Make and attach handles (one handle attached at points marked on each end) as shown in Chapter 3.

Mark and punch the body of the bag and fit in long gusset, as shown in Chapter 2, making sure that top centre points and sides are matched carefully before thonging.

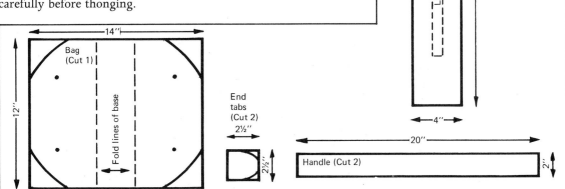

Sailcloth bag with leather trim

Requirements

Leather – 2 strips, each 18in by $\frac{1}{2}$in; 4 strips each 9in by $\frac{3}{4}$in. *Sailcloth* – (bought by the yard, 36in wide): 1 piece 18in by $9\frac{1}{2}$in, on double fold; 2 pieces each 5in by 4in, on double fold; 1 piece, 6in by 3in, for pocket. *Fittings* – 1 small Twinlock fastener; 4 small tubular rivets; Copydex adhesive.

To make bag

Cut out the large sailcloth piece on the fold, as shown in the diagram. One layer will form the outside and one layer the inside lining of the bag, and the folded line will be the upper front line of the bag, which goes under the flap.

Turn in $\frac{1}{4}$in hem all around on the pocket, and stitch. Now stitch the pocket to the inside layer of the large piece of sailcloth, so that it begins 2in below the fold line for front of bag. On the other layer (which will be the outside of the bag), $2\frac{1}{2}$in below the fold line, fix the lower part of the Twinlock fastener. Now, with the sailcloth still in the double fold, stitch the two layers together on the three open sides, turning in the edges $\frac{1}{4}$in to neaten, as you stitch.

Use adhesive to stick one 18in strip of leather evenly along each side and one 9in strip across each end. Machine-stitch the leather strips in place all around.

With the folded edge to the top and turning in the edges, stitch the two layers of each gusset together. Fit the gussets to the bag as shown in Chapter 2, but machine-stitch them in place instead of using thonging. Fix the upper part of the Twinlock fastener to the centre of the flap edge, as shown in diagram.

With wrong sides together, join the two remaining 9in leather strips to form the handle, using machine stitching. Use rivets to attach the ends of the handle to the top fold of the bag.

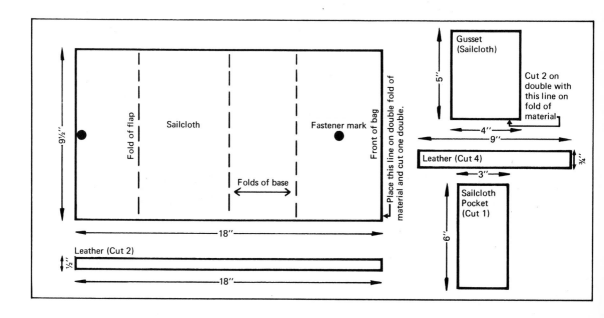

Two-tone shoulder bag

Requirements

Leather – 2 strips, each 23in by $\frac{1}{2}$in; 2 strips each 15in by $\frac{3}{4}$in; 1 strip, 9in by $\frac{1}{2}$in; 1 strip, 6in by $\frac{1}{2}$in; 2 gussets, each 7in by 3in, tapered at one end. *Patterned canvas* – 2 pockets, each 6in by 4in; 1 piece 23in by 9in, cut on double fold of material, as indicated in diagram. *Fittings* – 1 brass press-stud.

To make bag

Turn in and stitch double hem on one long side of canvas pockets, and turn in single $\frac{1}{4}$in hem on other three sides. Remembering that double fold of canvas represents front edge of bag, and following guidelines indicated on diagram, mark positions of press-studs on *outer* layer of canvas, and lines for pockets on *inner* layer, which is to be the lining. Stitch the pockets to the lining on back and front of bag.

Fix the underpart of the press-stud to the outside front. Stitch the two layers of canvas together, $\frac{1}{4}$in from edge around all edges. Now open the panel out flat and stitch one of the 23in strips of leather to each side on the outside of the panel, turning in the raw edge of the canvas $\frac{1}{4}$in at the same time. Stitch the 6in leather strip across the flap and the 9in strip across the fold at the front of the bag. You now have the entire outline of the bag covered with leather strips on the right side. Punch holes for thonging and thong gussets in position as shown in Chapter 2. Fix the top part of the press-stud to the flap of the bag.

Using the two 15in leather strips, make a strap. This can be longer or shorter than our version, according to taste. With the wrong sides of the strips facing each other, machine-stitch them together, $\frac{1}{4}$in from edge all round. Then, to trim, punch holes $\frac{1}{4}$in apart down the centre of the strap, and insert thonging in a running stitch down its length, leaving a length of thonging free at each end. Use thonging ends to attach strap to the top of each gusset.

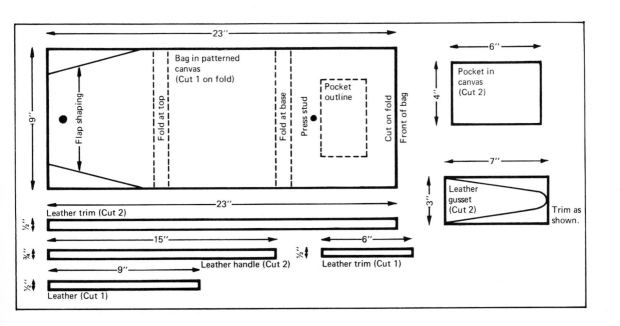

Ornate fold-over bag

A lightweight split with a firm, shiny surface was used for the roll effect on this bag. The edge trim is dressmakers' trim from the haberdashery department.

Requirements

Leather – 1 piece 25in by 10½in; 2 pieces, each 6½in by 3in, for gussets; 1 piece 24in by 1¼in, for strap handle; sufficient skiver leather, for lining, to line all the above pieces; 2 pockets (optional), each 5in by 5in, cut from lining leather. *Fittings* – 1 large press-stud; 5yd thonging; 1½yd 1in-wide decorative edge trim; 1 1in-wide gilt buckle, to fit trim; 4 decorative gilt rivets.

To make bag

Fix lower part of press-stud, as indicated in diagram. Stitch pockets (optional) to back and front of lining, stick lining to wrong side of bag panel and trim edges of lining.

On right side of bag panel, stick edge trim evenly along sides and machine-stitch in position. Fix top of press-stud to flap (see diagram). Thread buckle through trim and centre buckle over press-stud when attaching edge trim across end of flap. Punch edges of bag all round to fit lined gussets and thong as instructed in Chapter 2. Stitch edge trim to centre of strap and fix decorative rivets at points where trim ends. Line and thong the strap and use thonging to attach strap ends to tops of gussets on each side.

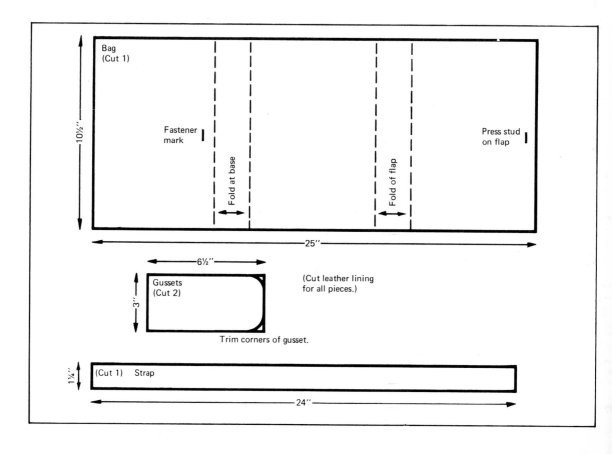

Writing case

Requirements

Leather – for outer part, 1 piece of strong but flexible leather, 18in by 12in; for lining and pockets, about twice the above amount, in a thin, flexible skiver; *Contrast trim* – 1 piece $1\frac{1}{2}$in by $5\frac{1}{2}$in, for strap, and 2 triangular pieces, for corners. *Fittings* – 1 press-stud; 3yd thonging; Copydex adhesive.

To make case

Cut out the lining to match the main piece, and cut pockets. Following diagram for inside of case, when completed, stitch stamp pocket to one of the smaller pockets. Matching sides and corners, stitch smaller pockets to large pockets with one centre row of stitches, as shown. Again matching sides and corners, stitch pockets to lining along sides.

Fix the lower part of press-stud to one side of the outer leather, as shown in diagram. Fix upper part of press-stud in contrast leather tab and stitch straight end of tab to edge of lining on opposite side.

Use adhesive to stick lining to outer leather and to stick corner tabs to corners of side to which underpart of press-stud is attached. Punch case all around through edges of lining, pockets and corner tabs, and insert thonging, to complete case.

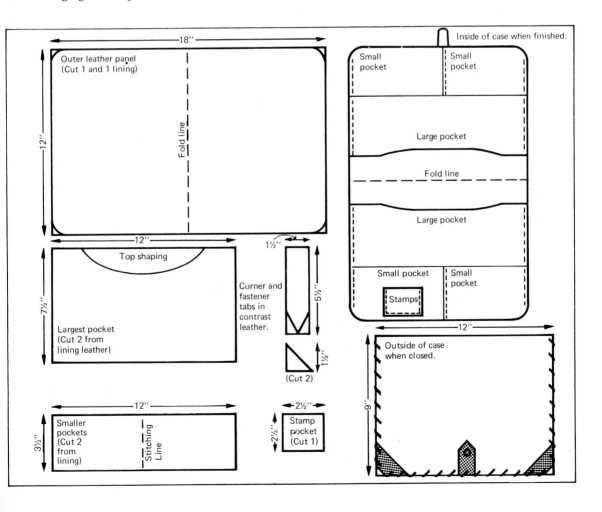

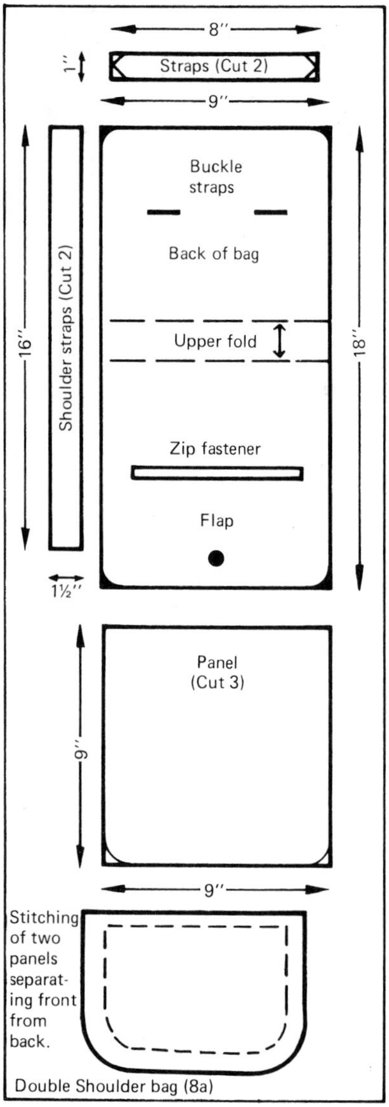

Shoulder bag with two compartments

Although this divided type of bag looks difficult, it is quite easy to make. We used a red split, with a lining in the same colour.

Requirements

You will need a skin measuring at least 4sq ft, and $\frac{1}{2}$yd of lining material, or a piece of skiver leather measuring 18in by 9in. It is best to use skiver, if you can. *Leather* to be cut as follows: 1 18in by 9in piece of outer leather (trim corners); 1 18in by 9in piece of lining, to match; 3 panels in outer leather, each 9in by 9in; 2 shoulder straps, each 16in by 1$\frac{1}{2}$in; 2 small straps, each 8in by 1in. *Fittings* – 5 1in-wide buckles; 15 eyelets, for straps; 2 D-rings and 2 dog-lead swivel clips; 6 tubular rivets; decorative motif or initial; 1 press-stud; 3yd thonging; 1 7in zip fastener.

To make bag

Before cutting other pieces, cut out shoulder strap, which can be cut in one long piece or two short pieces and joined by a buckle. Fold strap in two lengthwise and thong edges together. If using two pieces, attach buckle to one end and fit eyelets into other end.

Cut opening for zip in flap end of outer panel and stitch in zip, as shown in Chapter 3. Fix underpart of press-stud to flap end of outer panel, as shown in diagram, and fit in initial or other motif.

Cut 4 small tabs, each measuring 2in by 1in. Fit these to buckles and stitch (raw edges downwards) two of these to lower end of back at points shown in diagram. Stitch the two remaining buckles and straps to the lower end of one of the 9in by 9in panels, which will now be the front of the bag.

Use adhesive to stick lining to the back part of the large panel but not to the flap. Instead, stitch lining round edges of flap and across the top fold, 7in from lower edge of flap. This allows a pocket to be formed between lining and main leather part in front, opened by the zip fastener.

Now we return to the three 9in by 9in panels. The one with buckles attached will form the lower front of your bag. The other two are used to make the joining which divides the bag into two separate compartments. With wrong sides together and matching sides and corners, stitch these two panels together across the top edge to within 2in of each side. Stitch them together 2in from edge all round as shown in stitching detail.

The next step is to thong the front 9in by 9in panel round side and lower edge, to one of the joined panels, down sides and across lower end. Thong the back of the bag to the other side of the joining, and thong all round flap, to complete bag. Make the straps which are to unite back and front by thonging the two 8in by 1in strips round edges and fitting eyelets an even distance from point at each end.

To attach shoulder strap, insert two eyelets at each side of the top fold of the flap, so that eyelets are placed 1in apart and 1in from side of back. Fit a D-ring into each set of eyelets and fit the dog-lead swivels to the D-rings. To complete, attach a ring to each end of the shoulder strap already made.

Two-tone shoulder bag

For this bag we combined leather with sailcloth. When sailcloth is stuck to leather, the edges won't fray.

Requirements

Sailcloth – 1 piece 18in by 11in, for back and front; 1 piece 11in by 10½in, for flap (trim curves); 2 pieces, each 8½in by 2½in, for gussets; 1 piece 27in by 1½in, for shoulder strap. *Leather* – 1 piece, 11in by 10½in, to match sailcloth flap, and coloured leather scraps, for motif. *Lining* – Skiver or fabric lining to fit back and front and two gusset sections, and to make pockets. *Fittings* – 1 Twinlock fastener; 2 D-rings; 4 eyelet rivets.

To make bag

Trim leather for flap and stick to flap section cut in sailcloth, being careful to match curves and straight edges. Make and stick motif from coloured leather scraps to centre area of leather flap. Fit upper part of Twinlock fastener to edge of flap, and lower part to front panel. Make pockets and stick on lining to back and front of bag.

Stitch straight edge of flap along stitching line indicated on pattern, to back of bag. Line gussets and fit them to bag by thonging, as shown in Chapter 2. Thong bag neatly all around. To attach shoulder strap to bag, use rivets to attach D-rings to gussets, then attach ends of strap to D-rings.

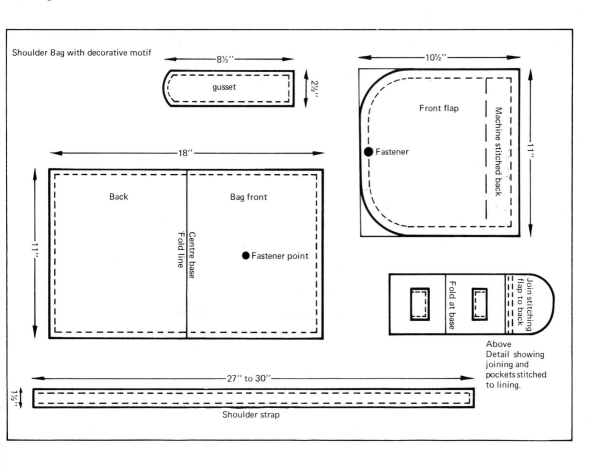

Decorated shoulder bag with zip

Requirements

We made this bag from a glossy 'processed' leather. The amount of leather required is about $3\frac{1}{2}$sq ft and the same amount of skiver for lining, cut as follows: 2 panels and 2 linings, each cut according to directions in diagram – trim all corners to curves; 1 base and 1 lining to match, measuring 12in by $4\frac{1}{2}$in; 2 gussets and linings to match, each $8\frac{1}{2}$in by $4\frac{1}{2}$in; scraps of coloured leather to make motifs. *Fittings* – 1 10in zip fastener; 4yd of thonging; buckle and eyelets for shoulder strap; Copydex adhesive.

To make bag

Using rubber-based adhesive, stick motifs to back and front panels. Stick lining to panels and trim lining edges. Being careful to match centres and sides of both panels, stitch zip to top edges of panels (see sewing diagram), according to instructions in Chapter 3. Mark and punch back and front panels and fit in lined base and gussets, as shown in Chapter 2, thonging bag neatly all round.

Stick lining to shoulder straps. Mark and thong straps all round and attach one end to the top of each gusset by thonging them together securely.

Attach buckle to free end of one shoulder strap and fit eyelets into the free end of the remaining strap, to allow adjustments.

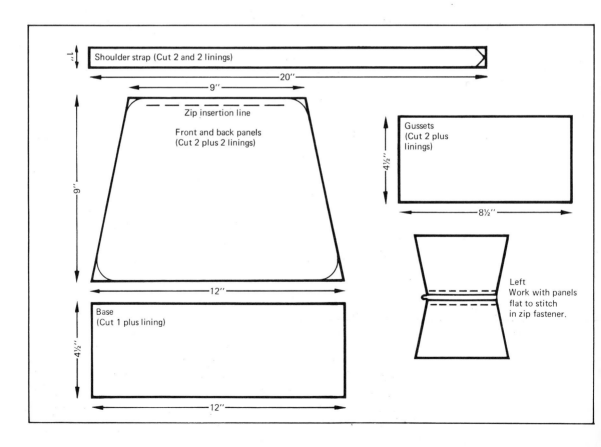

1″

Shoulder strap (Cut 2 and 2 linings)

20″

9″

Zip insertion line

Front and back panels
(Cut 2 plus 2 linings)

Gussets
(Cut 2 plus
linings)

4½″

8½″

6″

12″

Base
(Cut 1 plus lining)

4½″

12″

Left
Work with panels
flat to stitch
in zip fastener.

Shoulder bag with painted design

Requirements

Skin of light sheepskin, from which to cut the following: 1 piece 18in by 11in, shaped as shown in diagram, for back and flap combined; 1 shaped piece, 11in by 8in, for front of bag; 1 piece 24in by 4in, shaped as shown in diagram, to form 1 long gusset; 2 shoulder straps, each measuring up to 15in; lining to fit all pieces, preferably skiver.
Fittings – 1 press-stud or Twinlock fastener; 1 buckle, and eyelets.

To make bag

Follow directions given in Chapter 4 to model or paint a design on the outer leather of the flap. Fit upper part of fastener to lower end of the flap.

Fit underpart of fastener to handbag front, where indicated on diagram. Stick lining to back and front of bag, and gusset. Stitch straight edge of flap to upper edge of back.

Following the instructions given in Chapter 2, mark, fit and thong gusset to bag, and thong bag neatly all around. Stick lining to strap sections. Attach buckle to one strap and fit eyelets to pointed end of other strap. Use thonging to attach free ends of straps firmly to tops of gussets on each side.

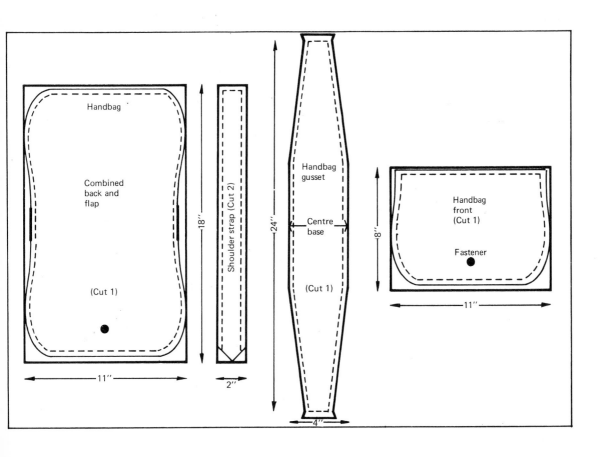

Bag with zip closure

For this bag we used a split with a glossy finish, and skiver leather for lining and pockets.

Requirements

Leather – 1 piece, 18in by 10in, for body of bag; 2 pieces each 7in by 4½in, for gussets; 1 piece 12in by 2½in, for zip fastener panel; 2 pieces each 18in by 1½in, for handles. *Lining* – enough for body of bag and gussets in same measurements, plus 2 pieces for pockets, each 7in by 4in. *Fittings* – 10in zip fastener; 2 lengths of handle cord, each 15in long and ¼in thick; Copydex adhesive.

To make bag

Fold each handle in two lengthwise. Punch sides and round the pointed ends, as shown in diagram. Leaving pointed ends open, thong each handle along its length, enclosing a length of cord at the same time.

On the back and front panels of the bag and in the positions indicated on diagram, mark for punching through holes already made in the pointed end of the handle (be careful to match the same handle end as used for marking). Punch holes in panel and attach handle ends by thonging neatly and fastening off thonging on wrong side of bag.

Stitch pockets to back and front areas of lining. Using rubber based adhesive, stick lining to body of bag and trim lining edges. Punch round edges. Line gussets, and fit to bag, as shown in Chapter 1, leaving top edges of bag free. Insert zip into top (12in by 2½in) panel, as shown in Chapter 3. Matching ends and centres, thong zip panel to top of bag, as shown in diagram, to complete.

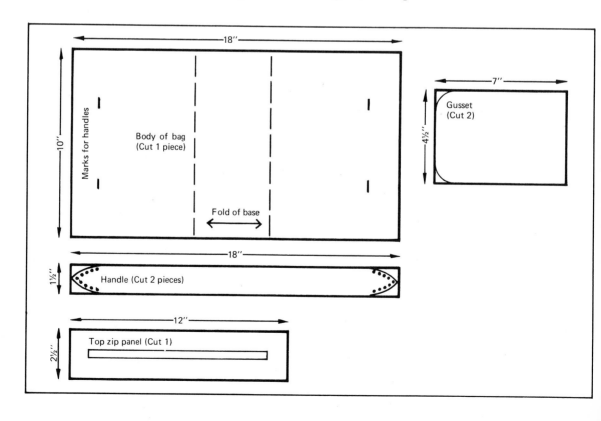

Painted evening bag

White lambskin was used for this bag, and the total requirement of leather was about 1½sq ft. For the lining a light leather fabric was bought by the yard – ¼yd of leathercloth is enough for this purpose.

Requirements
Leather – to be cut as follows: 1 large piece, 18in by 9in, for body of bag; 2 pieces, each 5½in by 1½in, for gussets; 1 piece 9in by ¾in, for handle. *Lining* – Skiver or leathercloth to match all leather pieces, plus sufficient to make 5in by 3½in pockets (optional). *Fittings* – 1 press-stud; 1½yd thonging.

To make bag
Decide on the motif you are going to use to decorate the bag, and trace out the design on the flap while you can still work with the leather completely flat. Follow the directions given for decorative work in Chapter 4. It is necessary to be careful when applying paints or dyes to the leather before the bag has been completed, to avoid the risk of staining other areas of the leather. Fit underpart of press-stud to front of bag, as indicated on diagram.

Make pockets in lining and stick lining to body of bag. Trim edges and punch all round. Line handle and stitch ¼in in from edge on both sides. Line gussets and fit to bag, as shown in Chapter 2. Catch in punched ends of handle at back of bag when thonging-in gussets, as shown in diagram.

To complete bag, fix upper part of press-stud to flap of bag, so that it will match lower part in front of bag.

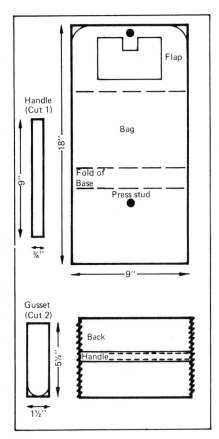

Belt and bag set

These could be made for evening wear in a silver or gilt-finish leather or leathercloth, or in more conventional types and shapes of light leather for ordinary wear.

Requirements
Leather – 1 piece measuring 20½in by 10in, for body of bag; 2 pieces, each measuring 7in by 2in, for gussets; 2 pieces, each measuring 18in by 2in, for belt (if length of leather permits, or you use a wide leather fabric, belt can be cut in one piece). *Lining* – Skiver leather, to line all the above pieces. *Fittings* – 1 turnlock fastener, for bag; ¾yd gilt chain, for bag; gilt buckle to fit 2in wide belt; 10 gilt eyelets (4 to fit chain to bag and 6 for belt); 2 gilt rings to attach chain to bag; 4 gilt tubular rivets; Copydex adhesive.

To make belt
Using a flat, overlapping seam (see Seams, Chapter 6), join the two belt pieces neatly. Use rubber-based adhesive to stick lining to belt. Trim one end of belt to a point and stitch on all edges, ¼in from cut edge. Punch hole 2in from straight end and fix eyelet in place, to fit prong of buckle. Machine-stitch end to belt, to hold buckle in place. At pointed end, mark for eyelet placement and punch and fit five eyelets, 1½–2in apart.

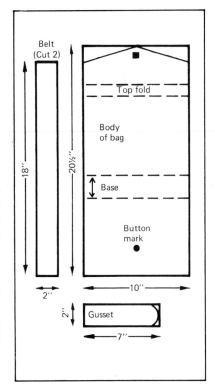

To make bag

Fit lower part of turnlock fastener to front of bag. Use adhesive to stick lining to main part of bag and to gussets. Fit gussets to bag, as shown in Chapter 2, and thong bag all around. Fit upper part of turnlock to flap of bag. Fit two eyelets 1in apart and $\frac{1}{2}$in from the top of each gusset and fit rings to catch chain through these.

A leather choker necklet

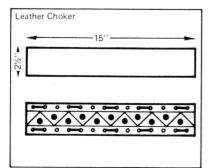

Leather Choker

For this choker, we used a strip of soft coloured leather, a Velcro fastening and decorative edge trim from the haberdashery department.

Requirements

Leather – 15in (or according to neck size) soft leather, $2\frac{1}{2}$in wide; *Trim* – 16in by $1\frac{1}{2}$in decorative trim or ribbon; *Backing* – 15in by $2\frac{1}{2}$in adhesive binding tape; *Thonging* to stitch choker; *Velcro* – 2in of 2in-wide Velcro, for fastening.

To make choker

Stitch trim to leather band, $\frac{1}{8}$in from edges, leaving a margin of $\frac{1}{2}$in on each side and allowing trim to extend $\frac{1}{2}$in beyond leather at each end.

Punch holes evenly, $\frac{1}{4}$in from edge of leather on each side. Insert row of decorative thonging on either side, allowing thonging to go into alternate holes on right side (or into every hole, if preferred) for decorative effect. Stick adhesive binding tape over back of band, turning ends of trim under tape for a smooth finish.

Stitch 1in strips of Velcro to each end of band, remembering that one strip must be attached to wrong side of band and one strip to right side, to form fastening.

Decorated shoulder bag

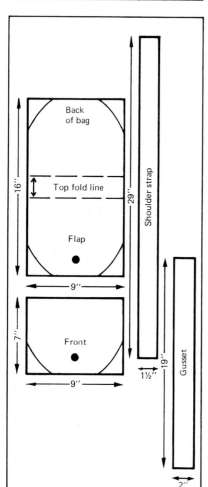

Made from lambskin with a motif painted on the flap, this bag requires about 2sq ft of leather, and an equal amount of skiver, for lining.

Requirements

Leather – 1 piece 16in by 9in, for back and flap; 1 piece 9in by 7in, for front of bag; 1 piece 19in by 2in, for gusset; 1 piece 29in by $1\frac{1}{2}$in (or 2 pieces each $14\frac{1}{2}$in by $1\frac{1}{2}$in) for shoulder strap. *Lining* – Skiver leather to match leather sections, plus 2 pieces each 6in by 4in, for pockets. *Fittings* – 1 press-stud or turnlock fastener; 2 rings, 4 eyelets and 2 rivets, for strap attachment; 1 buckle, $1\frac{1}{2}$in wide, if strap is cut in two pieces.

To make bag

Trace decorative design on flap, as explained in Chapter 4, but do not paint at this stage. Fit underpart of fastener to front of bag and upper part of fastener to flap, at points indicated on diagram. Stitch pockets to back and front linings.

Using rubber-based adhesive, stick lining to back and front bag sections, and gusset. Trim lining edges where necessary. Mark and

This suede outfit would make a very special gift for any child.

punch edges of back and flap section and of front. Matching centres and sides, mark and punch gusset to fit back and front sections. Paint design on flap and allow to dry completely.

Following directions given in Chapter 2, thong front of bag evenly to gusset. Fit two eyelets, $\frac{1}{2}$in apart and $\frac{1}{2}$in from top edge to each gusset, for strap attachment. Fit one ring on each side through the two eyelet holes.

If making strap in two sections, work each piece separately as follows: Stick lining to strap and machine stitch $\frac{1}{4}$in from edge all round. Punch one row of holes along centre of strap and thread strips of thonging in running stitch along sides of strap, to trim. Fit buckle to one strap. Trim one end of the other strap to a point and punch small holes at 1in intervals, for buckle prong.

Fit ends of shoulder strap through rings attached to gussets. Turn strap ends in and use decorative rivets to complete the joining.

Lastly, when painting on flap is completely dry, and being careful to match sides and centres of both as shown in Chapter 2, thong back and flap section of bag to gusset.

Shopping bag

This bag, which is made from soft basil, has six panels, made in alternating colours. Red and white has been used, but you can, of course, devise your own colour scheme. Apart from the base, the bag is unlined.

Requirements
Leather – 3 red pieces, each 13in by 6in, for panels; 3 white pieces, each 13in by 7in, for panels, 1 piece, 20in by 5in, for strap; 2 pieces, each $17\frac{1}{2}$in by $2\frac{1}{2}$in, for top binding; 1 piece 13in by 7in shaped to oval, for base. *Sailcloth* – 1 piece, 13in by 7in, to line base. *Fittings* – 1 piece of cardboard 12in by 6in, shaped to oval, to form base; 4 dome rivets, for base; 4 tubular rivets and 6 $\frac{1}{2}$in eyelets.

To make bag
(See instructions for working seams in Chapter 6). Leaving $\frac{1}{2}$in seam allowances throughout, and with right sides facing, machine-stitch the six alternating-coloured pieces together, along the 13in edge. Complete work at each point by flattening seam allowance and top-stitching $\frac{1}{4}$in from seam line on each side, and on right side of bag. When all pieces have been joined, the work will form a circle. Fit dome rivets to base, 2in from outer cut edge.

To fit leather to outer part of base, work with the circle you have constructed wrong side out, and the base wrong side out. Mark centre points of the base at sides and ends and use clothes pegs to hold the two edges together, when matching these points to the centre markings on the bag's lower edge. When you are satisfied that both parts fit evenly together, machine-stitch a seam $\frac{1}{2}$in from the cut edges, to join them. Trim the seam all round and clip notches from the curved edges, to remove excess bulk.

With right side of strip to wrong side of bag, and with the edges matching, stitch binding strip round top of bag. To complete the binding, overlap one end of strip over the other, trim excess material and stitch through all layers. Trim seam round top to $\frac{1}{4}$in. Turn strip to right side of bag and use clothes pegs to hold join flat round top edge.

Machine-stitch ¼in from raw edge all round.

To make strap, fold the 20in by 5in strip lengthways into three layers, as shown in cutting diagram. Machine-stitch round all edges and form ends into points. Use tubular rivets (two on each side) to fix handles to top binding of bag. Fit eyelets at intervals round binding of bag to trim.

Cover the oval-shaped cardboard piece with sailcloth and machine-stitch 1in from edge all round. Trim off surplus sailcloth. Finally, with smooth side of lining upwards, press stiffened lining into base of bag, so that it fits the shape of the base smoothly all round.

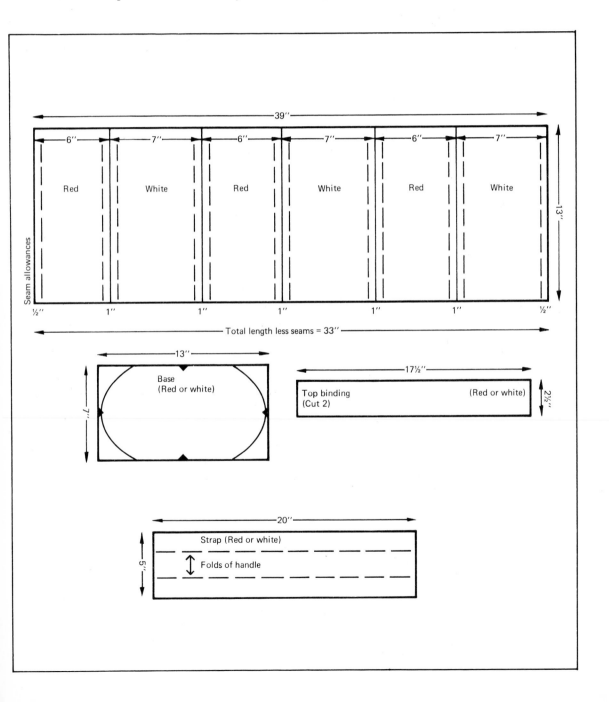

See page 75 for how to make the belt: the discs are cut from scraps and riveted together.

A sturdy little skirt with decorative seams and shiny buttons.

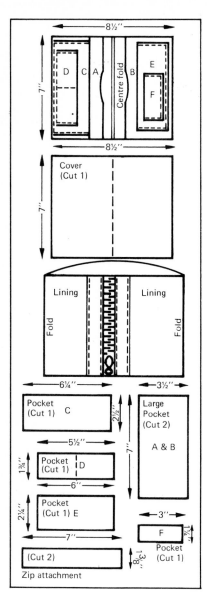

Man's wallet

Requirements
About 2sq ft of brown or black calf, pigskin, or stained basil, cut as follows: 1 piece 8½in by 7in, for wallet cover; 2 pieces, each 7in by 3½in, to form largest pockets (A and B); 1 piece, 6¼in by 2½in, to form pocket (C); 1 piece, 5½in by 1¾in, to form pocket (D); 1 piece, 6in by 2¼in, to form pocket (E); 1 piece, 3in by 1¼in, to form pocket (F); 2 pieces, each 7in by 1⅜in, for zip attachment. *Lining* – 1 piece of soft skiver leather, or lining fabric measuring 16in by 7in. *Fittings* – 1 7in zip fastener; 1yd thonging.

To make wallet
Following diagram, make pocket construction on each side, as follows:
For left side – machine-stitch pocket (D) to (C) and insert centre row of stitching, as shown, to divide pocket into stamp and ticket compartments. Now stitch (C) to (A) neatly round outer edges, so top remains open (see diagram).
For right-hand side – machine-stitch small pocket (F) to (E), and then stitch (E) to (B), so E forms another pocket.
Fit zip evenly to the edges of the two 7in by 1⅜in strips of leather, making sure that the ends of both leather strips are matching. Machine-stitch ¼in from edge on both.
Join lining to zip fastener by overlapping leather strips on lining and stitching ¼in in from edge on each side, as shown in diagram. As you can see from illustration, lining is now in two layers: one layer, to the centre of which zip is attached, will form the pocket into which the zip fastener opens; the second layer will form the true lining of the wallet, and should be stuck firmly to the wrong side of the 8½in by 7in wallet cover. When sticking lining, make sure that zip is correctly placed at centre fold.

To assemble wallet
Fit left-hand pocket structure (DCA) to left side and right-hand structure (BEF) to right side to lining as shown, using a light application of rubber-based adhesive to hold outer edges in place. Punch holes evenly all round through all thicknesses of leather and thong neatly to complete wallet.

Evening bag in simulated leather

As this bag is designed for occasional use, it seems a good idea to make it in one of the very attractive silver or gilt imitation leathers which can be bought by the yard. These, of course, are cheaper than real leather, but don't wear as well. We made it with a leather handle, but a gilt chain of similar length can be used instead.

Requirements
Leather cloth – 1 piece, 22in by 6in, shaped as shown in diagram, to form main part of bag; 2 pieces, each 6in by 2½in, to form gussets;

2 pieces, each 16in by 2in, for straps (optional) or 1 piece 30in by 2in (no strap needed if chain is being used). *Lining* – 1 piece of light skiver leather to fit main section of bag and 2 gussets, plus enough to make 2 small pockets. *Fittings* – 1 gilt or silver-type Twinlock fastener, to match bag; 1 1in buckle for strap or length of chain; 4 eyelets; 2 rings to attach strap or chain to gussets.

To make bag

Make pockets in lining. Fit upper part of fastener to flap and lower part to front of bag, and stick lining to main part of bag and gussets. Fit eyelets, 1in apart and $\frac{1}{2}$in from upper edge, to top ends of both gussets, for chain or strap attachment.

Punch holes all round edge of main part of bag. Mark, punch and fit gussets to match on each side of bag. Thong bag all round. Fit rings to ends of chain and attach rings to eyelets on gussets. Or fold strap in two lengthways, stitch on both sides, fit buckle and attach rings at ends, to fit gusset tops.

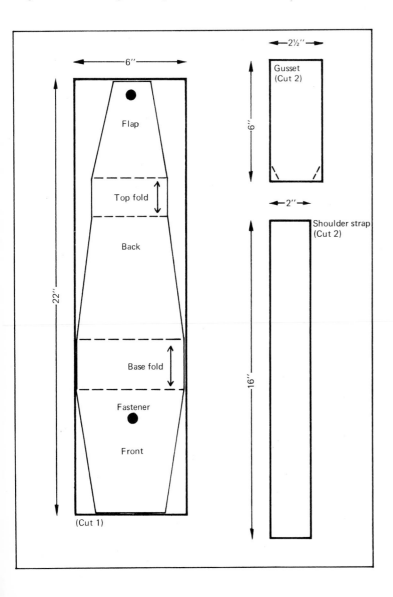

We made this suede waistcoat, and so.can you! The pattern and instructions are on pages 69 to 72.

*This tough red and white shopping bag will last forever. Make it from
our instructions on page 50.*

Collection of small gifts

Various small gifts can easily be made from the inevitable scraps accumulated during the course of leatherwork. Here are suggestions for some useful articles.

(1) Brush case

Cut one piece 8in by 4in, for back, one piece 4in by 4in, for front; one piece 4in by 2in, for base, and two pieces each 4in by 2in, for gussets. Cut lining material to fit all pieces. *Fittings* – 1 press-stud, and thonging.

Fit lower part of press-stud to front of case. Line all pieces and fit upper part of fastener to flap, as shown. Punch back and front sections all round, and fit base. Fit gussets, as shown in Chapter 2, and thong all round, to complete.

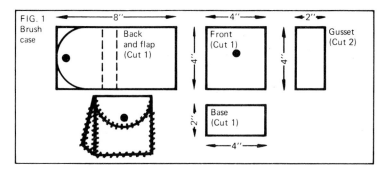

(2) Child's purse (unlined)

Cut one piece, 8in by 3in. Trim one end to form flap and fold piece, as shown in diagram. Fit press-stud as indicated, thong sides together and thong flap, to complete.

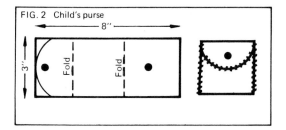

(3) Child's purse with zip

Cut two pieces, each 5in by 3in. Matching both pieces at sides, stitch on 4in zip fastener, as shown in diagram. With right sides out, double purse over, as shown. Trim off corners. Thong pieces together along sides and lower edge.

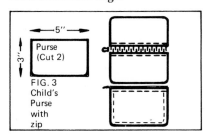

(4) Child's comb case

Cut two pieces, each 5in by 1½in and shape top and end as shown. Stitch or thong both together. Thong or stitch round curved edge at top, to give neat appearance.

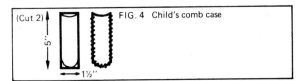

FIG. 4   Child's comb case

(5) Child's needle case

Cut a piece of leather, 8in by 3in and cut lining to match. Shape ends, as shown, and attach lower part of press-stud to front area of outer leather. Make small pockets to hold thread cards, etc. on lining, and stitch a 2in square of flannel or flannelette to centre area, to hold needles. Stick lining to back, thong round edges and fit upper part of press-stud to flap.

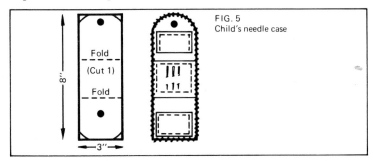

FIG. 5
Child's needle case

(6) Key case

Cut two pieces of leather, each 6in by 3in (one to be used as back and one as lining of case). Fit lower part of press-stud to front of case, as shown in diagram. Use rivets to attach key-ring fitting to centre area of lining. Thong round edges and fit upper part of press-stud to flap.

It is a good idea never to discard leather scraps. Even the smallest ones may be useful for stick-on or sew-on appliqué, when you are making a toy animal or some article in scrap-work. And, by the way, it is worth knowing that you can often buy a bundle of larger scraps from a leather merchant. These are sold by weight and priced according to quality.

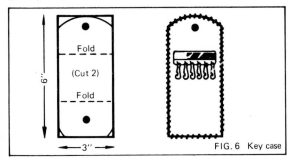

FIG. 6   Key case

These useful small items can all be made from leather scraps.
Instructions are on page 54 (wallet) and 58–59 (smaller items).

Attractive belts like these are easy to make – why not follow them with the bag? Instructions for the bag are on page 42.

6 Dressmaking

WEARABLES IN LEATHER

Nowadays when leather has really come into its own as a high fashion dressmaking material, you are bound to want to try your hand at making a garment. Certainly, leather is an expensive material to use in dressmaking, and for that reason you must be very careful to avoid costly mistakes. However, once you have mastered the art of sewing leather, you can make up attractive wearable clothes for a fraction of what they would cost to buy ready-made.

START WITH A PLAN

Plan your operation carefully and you are half-way to success. Decide what type of material you are going to use. For clothing you will need soft leather or soft suede, and we will tell you about the various types available presently. It's also worth remembering that most of the rules which apply to real leather also apply to simulated leather. Imitations can look good, though they are not as beautiful as the real thing, of course. But they are cheaper and can be bought by the yard, which is a decided advantage.

The next thing to decide is what you are going to make. Start with something simple – a sleeveless garment, for example, like the one we show you how to make – and make sure that your pattern is cut on straightforward lines. No matter how experienced you become, it is always wise to choose simple designs, with as few seams and sewing details as possible, when you work with leather.

TYPES OF SKIN AVAILABLE

Most of the soft, supple leathers and suedes used for clothing come from the sheep or cow. Both of these types are available in a wide variety of finishes and colours, so that you can buy embossed, 'antique', snakeskin and crocodile leathers and others which are in reality specially treated cow or sheep.

Sheep

Basically, this is the least expensive and most commonly used of the soft leathers. It is available in soft, pliable leathers and in beautiful velvet-like suedes. You can use it for skirts, jackets, coats, trousers and accessories.

Cow

Hide is the name given to the heavier leather obtained from the cow. However, the cow also provides lighter types of leather, one of these being suede 'splits' which can be used to make hard-wearing clothes. Another kind of leather obtained from this source is calfskin – a fine, supple leather used in coats and accessories.

Goatskin

Usually firmer in texture than sheepskin, goatskins are small supple skins suitable for fine garments. One of the commonest uses is in the making of gloves. One variety is called 'Morocco', a name associated with a particular dyeing and finishing process, and not related to the leather's country of origin.

Pigskin

This is one of the more expensive types of leather. You can tell real pigskin from imitations by the fact that the groups of small holes which characterise it go right through the leather and are not symmetrical, as in the machine-made pattern. The pig provides us with a fine silky suede which is suitable for garments, but it is best not to use this costly material until you have gained in experience.

Suede

Although we are including suede as a 'type' of leather, this doesn't come from one particular animal. It is a soft leather which has been specially treated on the flesh side to give it a velvety pile finish. The weight and texture of this material depend on its origin and the processes used in its manufacture.

Leather fabrics

The variety and quality of leather-like fabrics which copy the latest look in real leather is increasing. You will find many attractive finishes, especially in simulated 'antique' and 'wild' leathers, among these. As mentioned earlier, leather fabrics have advantages: they can be bought by the yard, are of the same weight and texture all over and cost less than the real thing.

WHEN YOU BUY LEATHER

This is one of your most important tasks. You are buying an expensive material and so you must choose wisely. The first essential is that you must know what you want. However helpful the salesman wishes to be, he can't tell you how much leather you need unless he has a clear idea of the way in which you are going to use it. So let him see the pattern you are going to use and take time in making your choice. Let us assume that you are going to make the waistcoat shown in the diagram, and see what points need to be watched:

1. Because the waistcoat is made from two small suede skins, check that both match in colour and weight, and that when combined, they are large enough.
2. Because suede has a pile, like velvet, make sure that all the pattern pieces can be cut out so that the pile is going in the same direction in all of them.
3. Because a skin of leather is uneven in shape and texture, it is necessary to check that all the pattern pieces can be cut from unflawed suede of even thickness.

Since leather is sold by the sq ft, and you will usually need more than one skin to make a garment, try to avoid waste as much as possible. Occasionally, you may be able to buy a matching half skin, but mostly you will find only whole skins on offer. So, while being careful to choose skins that are large enough, don't buy those that are larger than you need. Inevitably, you will have some waste scraps left over anyway.

This friendly spotted dog, in white basil with dark spots, is easy to make – instructions on page 79.

Never throw these away, for they can be used to effect in leather patchwork, as we show later.

STORING LEATHER BEFORE USE

Leather creases easily and should not be folded. Note the way in which leather is stored in the shop: to avoid creasing, it is kept hanging or completely flat.

THE RIGHT KIND OF PATTERN

Some pattern manufacturers supply a limited number of styles which are especially recommended for leather. However, once you have grasped the essentials of working with this new material, you will see that it is easy to adapt ordinary patterns which are suitable in other respects.

Watch out for styles which have as few seams, darts and fitted panels as possible. Start with a simple straight skirt or sleeveless garment. Later, when you have gained experience, you will be pleased to discover that because of the stretchable quality of leather, sleeves can be set in quite easily, but they are best avoided in the beginning.

Adjusting pattern for fitting

Having chosen your pattern in the right size, make a careful check to see what fitting adjustments are necessary, before starting to cut the leather. This is very important because needle marks will show on the finished garment if you have to rip out seams. The only sure way to cope with fitting problems in advance is to make a muslin replica of the garment first.

This extra trouble and the small expense involved are well worthwhile when you are using a costly fabric like leather. However, you don't need to finish the garment in muslin: all you need do is to make any darts that are in the design and join up all the main seams, being careful to take in the correct seam allowance. Then if you find that there are faults in the fitting, make a note of these and mark your pattern to allow for any adjustments necessary.

Normally, if the pattern is in the correct size for you, fitting adjustments of this kind should be very simple. For example, the length may be wrong – a matter which can easily be corrected. If the width is too narrow, then the best way to solve this problem is to add width at the side seams. If the garment is too wide, increase the seam allowance at the side seams from, say, $\frac{5}{8}$in to 1in. Shapings can be corrected by increasing or decreasing the size and length of darts. However, do remember that if you find any major adjustments are necessary, your measurements are probably wrong and the pattern size is not correct for you.

Marking the leather

Work with the leather right side down on a large, flat, clean surface: a large piece of hardboard placed on a table with the smooth side up makes a very good working surface. Each pattern piece must be cut out separately in a single thickness of leather, so take extra care when you have to cut out two back or two front sections of a garment or two sleeves. For if you are not careful, you could easily end up with two left or two right fronts, back sections or sleeves!

Since most patterns are designed for cloth which is to be cut on the double, this is a real danger. The best way to avoid it is to cut a duplicate of each pattern piece, check the two pieces to see that they match correctly, and then mark each very clearly with a 'right side up' indication.

Another point to bear in mind is that the pile of suede should go in the same direction on all pattern pieces – something you could forget when the suede is face downward. Failure to place the pattern pieces correctly could result in variations in shading in the finished garment.

Do not pin the pattern pieces to the leather, as you would do in the case of a cloth fabric. Instead, use strips of transparent sticky tape or masking tape to hold the pattern sections in place. Use a light pencil or French chalk to transfer pattern markings to the wrong side of the leather. Don't cut the leather until you are satisfied that all pattern pieces have been placed correctly on the leather.

If you run short of leather

No matter how well you think you have planned your operation, it is possible to run short at the last minute. You will probably make this discovery when you set out your pattern pieces, and may well find that, though you have enough material in terms of square feet, the area is not of the proportions necessary to allow you to cut all your pattern sections in one piece.

Don't despair. Provided that enough material is there, you can overcome this problem in various ways. For instance, if there isn't enough leather for a one-piece back, have a centre-back join, but do remember to add on ½in seam allowance on each section. Another solution to the same problem would be to have a joining across the back, so that you get a yoke effect. In this case, be careful to add extra for seam allowances, and ensure that the alteration does not affect the shaping and size of the armholes.

These extra seams are often necessary in the making of leather clothes, because of the size and shape of the skin. Provided that joinings are made neatly and correctly centred, they can even give a decorative effect. We did tell you to avoid patterns which have too many *fitted* joinings, but that is a different matter altogether! Here are some guidelines to help you avoid the need for too many joinings:

Average skin sizes
Sheep: 7sq ft, 3½ft by 2ft, approximately.

Calf: 12sq ft, 4ft by 3ft, approximately.

Cow: 17sq ft, 5ft by 3½ft, approximately.

Garment requirements (approximate) of 7sq ft skins

Straight skirt Waistcoat	} 2 skins
Long-line jerkin Long-line waistcoat	} 3 skins
Coat Sleeveless trouser suit	} 8 or 9 skins

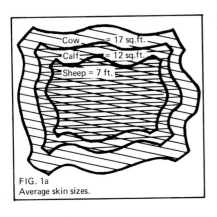

FIG. 1a
Average skin sizes.

CUTTING OUT YOUR GARMENT
For straight lines, use a leather knife and a ruler. For other lines, use sharp shears. Leave pattern pieces attached to leather as you cut and place all leather pieces lying flat, until you are ready to use them.

Getting ready to sew

Since leather can't be pinned or tacked, you need some other method for holding sections of your garment together for seaming. Sticky tape may be useful in areas where there isn't much strain, but where there is strong pressure needed to hold the parts in place, use paper clips or clothes pegs to grip the edges inside the seam allowance.

Before you start to sew, test your machine thoroughly on waste scraps of leather. A special leather needle is best, but you can manage quite well with an ordinary needle in size 14 or 16. It is best to start with a new needle.

Set your machine for 8 to 10 stitches per inch. Tension should be slightly loose, and a light machine pressure is best for most leathers.

Silk thread is suitable for machining thin leathers, but linen or 'heavy duty' mercerised thread is usually best for heavier types. You will find that hand-stitching is easier if you wax the thread, using candle or beeswax.

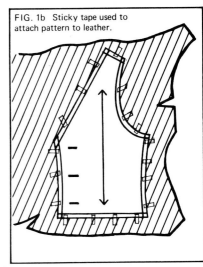

FIG. 1b Sticky tape used to attach pattern to leather.

Sewing seams

Because of the nature of leather, you will often find it easier to manage if you place a layer of tissue paper between the leather and the presser foot of the machine. This can be torn away when stitching has been completed. However, it is often advisable to 'stay' seams with ribbon seam binding (especially on curved and front edges), in which case you can stitch the binding in place as you go along, and may not need to use tissue paper.

Instead of using a back-stitch to secure ends of seams, as you might do with cloth, tie the upper and bobbin threads securely together at each end of the seam.

It is best to think of your seam allowance in terms of the standard $\frac{5}{8}$in used in dressmaking. You can then do any trimming necessary to reduce bulk afterwards. It is sometimes recommended that the seam allowance be reduced *in the pattern*, but it is best not to do this until you have gained experience.

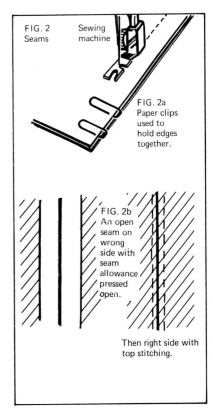

FIG. 2 Seams   Sewing machine

FIG. 2a Paper clips used to hold edges together.

FIG. 2b An open seam on wrong side with seam allowance pressed open.

Then right side with top stitching.

Open seams

To join two leather sections together (the side seams of our waistcoat, for instance), follow the steps shown in *Fig. 2*, as follows:

1   Use clips or clothes pegs to hold the pieces firmly together with right sides facing each other. Stitch as you would for a plain, flat seam in cloth fabric. Remember your work will be easier if you place a layer of tissue paper between leather and presser foot; or stitch seam binding to the two layers of leather as you go along. Remove clips or pegs as you complete stitching.

2   You cannot effectively press natural or artificial leather, for fear of damaging the material. However, it will help to flatten and press the seam open if you use a warm, dry (but not hot) iron over a dry pressing cloth on the wrong side of the garment.

3   Leather seams will not lie flat of their own accord, so they should always be top-stitched on the right side: to do this, insert a neat, even row of machine stitches $\frac{1}{4}$in from the seam joining on each side. If you have difficulty in getting seam allowances to lie flat for top-stitching, a problem which can arise when you are dealing with thicker leathers, use a hammer covered with cloth to tap the seam allowances flat. Use a rubber adhesive such as Copydex very sparingly to stick seam allowances to the wrong side of the material.

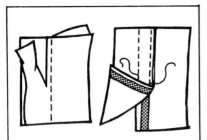

FIG. 2c Flat-fell seam details. On wrong side one edge is trimmed. Then on right side seam is top stitched. (Shaded area represents rubber adhesive.)

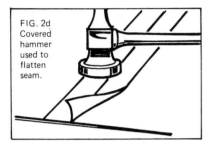

FIG. 2d Covered hammer used to flatten seam.

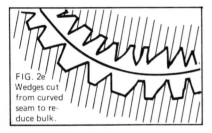

FIG. 2e Wedges cut from curved seam to reduce bulk.

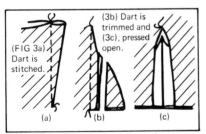

(FIG 3a) Dart is stitched.

(3b) Dart is trimmed and (3c), pressed open.

(a)   (b)   (c)

Flat-fell seams

Essentially, this type of seam is made in leather in the same way as for cloth fabric *except* that, with leather, you usually have one raw edge showing. You may find this easier than the open seam described on page 67 for some operations:

1 Follow directions given in Step 1 above, for open seams.
2 Trim one seam allowance edge to $\frac{1}{4}$in along its entire length. Open the garment out so that the joining is flat and lap the untrimmed seam allowance over the trimmed edge.
3 Use a covered hammer to tap the lapped edge flat and then use rubber adhesive lightly to keep the lapped edge in place. Top-stitch neatly close to the raw edge. To complete seam, insert second row of stitching about $\frac{1}{2}$in from the first.

Corners and curves

The important thing in getting a neat finish throughout your work is to eliminate unnecessary bulk. On concealed seams, such as joinings on the insides of collars, clip corners and trim off seam allowances to $\frac{1}{4}$in before turning collar right side out. On curved seams which are to be pressed open, cut out small V-shaped wedges before flattening the seam.

Darts

Stitch dart in the normal way on the wrong side of the material. Tie threads securely at both ends. Trim off the material taken up in dart to $\frac{1}{4}$in. On wrong side, use padded hammer to press seam allowance on dart open; and use rubber adhesive sparingly to secure the edges to the garment. For extra support, top-stitch evenly along each edge of dart, as shown in *Fig. 3*.

Hems

Trim hem allowance to not more than 2in. Fold hem up on wrong side and use rubber adhesive to hold it in place. Then tap with a padded hammer to flatten fold. If you are using a lining, you can then stitch the raw edge of the hem to it. However, for additional security, you may prefer to machine-stitch the hem neatly all round. When dealing with a curved hem, cut out small V-shaped wedges to reduce bulk, as in the case of a curved seam.

Facings, linings and interlinings

Use a non-woven iron-on interlining, such as Vilene, for front edges etc, and use a *warm* iron over brown paper to press it in place. Because of pressing difficulties, it is advisable to top-stitch all edges on right side, for a neat finish. You will have noticed that leather garments tend to have a lot of top-stitching for a useful and decorative effect.

Buttons and buttonholes

For extra support, always stitch a shirt button on the wrong side of the garment and directly underneath the large button, stitching through both at the same time.

Handworked or machine-worked buttonholes are not suitable for leather or leather fabrics. The best type to use is a bound buttonhole; if you are not experienced in this technique, practise making bound buttonholes on scraps of the leather you are using:

1 Mark but do not cut the positions of buttonholes on the right side

of the garment. For each buttonhole, cut two strips of leather, each 1½in in width and ½in longer than the required buttonhole.

2 Fold the strips in two lengthwise, with right side out. Use a covered hammer to flatten the fold and rubber adhesive to hold the edges of strip together.

3 Stitch one strip to garment above and below buttonhole marking, so that raw edges meet at marking line. Stitching should be not more than ¼in from raw edges.

4 Using your ruler and knife and with the garment placed on a flat surface, cut the buttonhole between the two strips of binding. Clip leather into each of the four corners, as shown in *Fig. 4*.

5 Gently draw bindings to wrong side of garment through slit, and arrange them evenly so that rim of binding is straight on right side. Stitch the ends of binding together by hand on wrong side.

6 On right side, top-stitch buttonhole ¼in from edge of opening all round.

(FIG 4a). On right side, binding is stitched above and below buttonhole marking. (4b). Shows buttonhole cut on wrong side. (4c). Binding drawn to wrong side and ends stitched. (4d) Shows top-stitching on right side. (4e). Shows lining cut and stitched to binding on wrong side.

Instructions for lady's waistcoat (1 sq = 1in)

Our pattern, page 70, is size 12, to fit bust 34in, and 1 sq = 1in. To alter the pattern to a smaller size (10) or a larger size (14) deduct or add 2in all round. You can make these alterations before cutting out your pattern by re-drawing the pattern sections on squared grid paper.

Altering size

The smaller diagrams show where size may be altered. Because any change usually involves reducing or enlarging the armhole, you should alter its size also, on the diagrams. Follow these guidelines:

Each of the two pattern pieces represents one-quarter of the garment. So to subtract or add 2in all round means altering each of the two sections by ½in only.

Therefore to make an alteration which enlarges the armhole and gives slightly more width at the shoulder line, you need only extend the pattern sections by ¼in on each piece.

Length

Because length is not always related to size, this is something you will need to check against your own measurements. Or you may wish to make the waistcoat longer or shorter than our pattern allows. On the small diagrams we have indicated the position (at the waistline) where length can be altered.

Seam allowances

Unless otherwise indicated these are ⅝in. For the centre-back joining we have allowed ½in seam allowance, but if you have enough leather to allow you to cut the back out in one piece, this should be eliminated. On the other hand, if you find you need to make extra joins because the skins are not the right shape, be careful to add an extra ½in where joins are being made.

Making the pattern

Use a ruler or yardstick to measure out rectangles of the size shown in our diagrams, on firm paper. Still using the ruler and following our

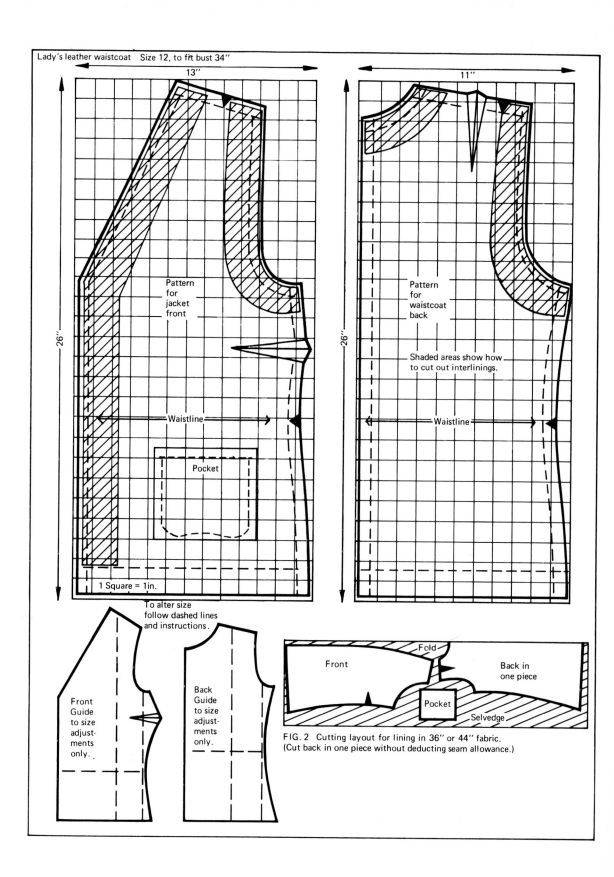

Lady's leather waistcoat   Size 12, to fit bust 34"

13"

Pattern
for
jacket
front

26"

Waistline

Pocket

1 Square = 1in.

11"

Pattern
for
waistcoat
back

Shaded areas show how
to cut out interlinings.

26"

Waistline

To alter size
follow dashed lines
and instructions.

Front
Guide
to size
adjust-
ments
only.

Back
Guide
to size
adjust-
ments
only.

Front

Fold

Back in
one piece

Pocket

Selvedge

FIG. 2 Cutting layout for lining in 36" or 44" fabric.
(Cut back in one piece without deducting seam allowance.)

measurements (remember each square is equal to 1in), draw the pattern in pencil inside the diagram. Fill in the outlines and positions of darts and pockets, but ignore the lines which indicate interlinings at this stage. Draw in curves at armholes and on pockets.

Check all measurements carefully before cutting out the pattern. To avoid confusion when you have to cut out the leather, cut two front and two back patterns and mark each 'right' or 'left' as appropriate, very clearly. If you can cut the waistcoat back all in one piece, then cut the pattern for the back in one piece also.

To avoid fitting problems and mistakes later, cut out a muslin version of the waistcoat first. Make darts and join seams before fitting. Only when you are satisfied that the waistcoat will fit well should you cut the leather. To cut out the garment, follow the instructions given earlier.

Requirements

Leather – 2 to 3 suede skins, each measuring 7sq ft. We used two sheep suede skins, but if you want a longer or larger-size waistcoat, you may need more leather than this. *Lining* – $\frac{3}{4}$yd 36in-wide non-woven interlining, such as Vilene; $1\frac{1}{2}$yd 36in-wide medium-weight cloth lining fabric; *Fittings* – Fancy hook fastener for edge-to-edge front closure (optional); seam binding; sewing thread; rubber adhesive, such as Copydex.

Sewing instructions

For details such as darts, seams and hems, follow the directions given earlier in this chapter. Cut lining out so that it is identical with jacket sections. Cut pocket lining.

To make waistcoat

1 Make bust darts in front.
2 With right sides of leather and lining together, stitch pocket to pocket lining, leaving top edge free to turn pocket right side out. With pocket right side out, turn in top edges of leather and lining, and machine across top edge $\frac{1}{4}$in from fold. Make second row of stitching $\frac{1}{2}$in from the first, across top of pocket.
3 Working slowly and carefully, attach pockets to fronts, along marking lines indicated on pattern, by stitching $\frac{1}{4}$in from edge along sides and lower end.
4 Make shoulder darts in back. Join back sections at centre back seam, unless back is cut in one piece.
5 Following the interlining areas indicated on diagrams, draw interlinings for front, back neck and armholes on back and front patterns. Trace these drawings carefully on a separate sheet of paper, cut these out and use them as patterns to cut out interlining material.
6 Working with garment sections face downward on a clean, flat surface, use rubber adhesive sparingly to stick interlinings evenly to front and neckline, as shown in *Figs. 1a* and *1b*, on wrong side of garment.
7 Using a flat, overlapping seam, stitch back and front armhole facings together at shoulder and underarms. Stitch the back to front sections of waistcoat at shoulder and underarm seams. Stitch underlinings carefully in place.
8 *Lining:* Stitch darts in front sections and press them downwards. Stitch shoulder darts in back and press these towards centre. With right sides together, fold back and make a $\frac{1}{2}$in-wide tuck, stitched

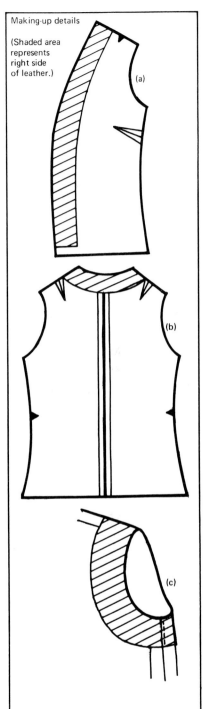

Making-up details

(Shaded area represents right side of leather.)

(a)

(b)

(c)

FIG. 1a Interlining attached to waistcoat after bust dart has been completed;
1b Interlining attached to back neckline after shoulder darts and back seam have been completed. 1c Interlining attached to armhole after shoulder and side seams have been completed.

$1\frac{1}{2}$in downward from neckline at centre back. Press. With right sides together and using ordinary flat seams, stitch the back to front lining sections at shoulder and side seams. Press all seams open.

9 *To line waistcoat:* With right sides together and matching seamlines, join lining to waistcoat at front edges. (Sew seam binding on *straight* edge). Use clips or pegs to hold the two layers of material together, and stitch $\frac{5}{8}$in from edge. Trim seam allowance and turn waistcoat right side out.

Turn in to wrong side and tack seam allowance on armholes of lining. Turn in to wrong side seam allowance on armhole of garment, using covered hammer to flatten the fold. Cut out V-shaped wedges from curves and use rubber adhesive to hold seam allowance in place. Then, matching seamlines, stitch lining to armhole of garment on right side: machine-stitch $\frac{1}{4}$in from edge and insert second row of stitches all round armhole, $\frac{1}{2}$in in from the first.

To complete waistcoat

Turn up $1\frac{1}{2}$in to 2in hem on waistcoat and use rubber adhesive to hold it in place.

Trim lower edge of lining and turn up a hem that is of sufficient depth to make lining 1in shorter than waistcoat. Machine-stitch and press lining hem.

Being careful to attach lower edges of lining neatly to waistcoat edges, top-stitch entire front edge of waistcoat by machine-stitching $\frac{1}{4}$in from edge on right side. Make second row of stitches $\frac{1}{2}$in from the first all round.

Optional finish: Using hand stitches, attach decorative edge fastenings to front edges. The waistcoat shown has one hook fastener at waist level, but you could use three fasteners placed $3\frac{1}{2}$in to 4in apart on straight front edge.

Gloves

Hand-made leather gloves have always been high fashion but, unfortunately, far too expensive for most of us. Now, you can learn how easy it is to make your own for a fraction of the cost in the shop – this is not nearly as difficult as you may think.

The best way to set about glovemaking is to buy a pattern for gloves in your size and of a design that appeals to you. However, it is best to choose a pattern on simple, classic lines, without unnecessary detail. The next step is to buy sufficient gloving leather. Your choice of leather is important, so ask the salesman to help you select either a natural chamois or a fine gloving suede.

When you come to copying your glove pattern on to the wrong side of the leather, be particularly careful to see that you have a left-hand and a right-hand glove: turn the pattern upside down to cut the second glove.

The standard glove pattern is cut in one piece with finger shapings and an opening for the thumb. The extras which have to be cut out include a thumb piece and gussets, and these have to be cut very accurately. Accuracy is essential also when joining up the various pieces, as any discrepancy will show and result in a bad fit.

Gloving needles, which have triangular points, are best for stitching heavier varieties of gloving leather, but a fine sewing needle can be used for chamois or fine suede. This is a task for hand sewing, so you will need time and patience to give the work the attention it needs. The most suitable threads are buttonhole twist and mercerised cotton, and if you wax the thread slightly, this will help.

Most hand-stitched gloves are sewn on the right side throughout. The two types of stitch most commonly used are the stab-stitch and a technique known as 'round seaming'.

Stab-stitching looks like a running stitch but shouldn't be confused with it. The major difference is in the way in which the two types of stitch are worked. In the case of running stitch, several stitches may be taken up on the needle at a time, but with stab-stitching one stitch is done at a time. For each stitch the needle is inserted through the two thicknesses of material and the thread is drawn up firmly. Stab-stitches should be about $\frac{1}{16}$in in length, placed $\frac{1}{16}$in from the edge (see *Fig. 1*).

Round seaming, which is an alternative method of joining glove sections, is basically oversewing, but with the needle going through each hole a second time. *Fig. 2* shows how this stitch is worked and how it should look.

Decorative stitching on the back of each hand, as shown in *Fig. 3*, is a simple running stitch. Here the guidelines are drawn in very lightly, the needle picks up one thickness of material at a time in a tiny stitch, and the thread is drawn up firmly, but not tightly to give a raised effect.

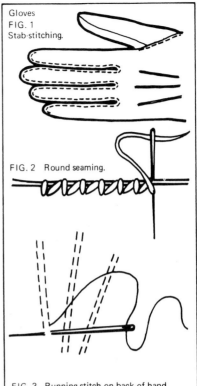

Gloves
FIG. 1
Stab-stitching.

FIG. 2 Round seaming.

FIG. 3 Running stitch on back of hand.

Moccasin slippers

Moccasin slippers are very easy to make. You can follow our diagram (1 sq = 1in) to cut out a pattern, in which case your slipper will be in size 6. For sizes above or below size 6, increase or decrease the pattern by $\frac{1}{2}$in per size in length and toe width. Or, following the same principle in making the slipper, make a pattern to fit your own foot, as follows:

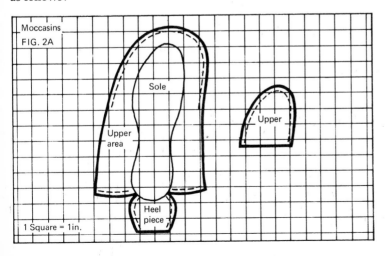

Moccasins
FIG. 2A

Sole

Upper

Upper
area

Heel
piece

1 Square = 1in.

Place your foot on a sheet of paper placed on a firm surface and draw in the outline all around. Then, for a slipper that will fit comfortably, add 1½in to the pattern all around. You will then have to draw in the heel piece and the upper area of the slipper, as shown.

Cut the entire slipper and the smaller upper piece shown in the diagram from a light, soft leather. Then, using the outline for the sole, cut out a sole slightly larger than this from light sole leather. Glue this firmly to the under-surface of the slipper, before stitching.

Join the upper pieces at the heel, as indicated. Then, using an oversewing stitch or light thonging, join the front upper sections. You will find that the upper 'apron' is smaller than the surrounding area into which it is to be fitted. The way to deal with this is to run gathering stitches through the surrounding area and draw these up evenly until the apron fits.

When making slippers you must remember to cut out the leather so that you have a right and left foot: when you have cut out one slipper, turn the pattern upside down to cut the next. And, as an added precaution, cut the pattern out in tissue paper and fit it to your foot before cutting the leather.

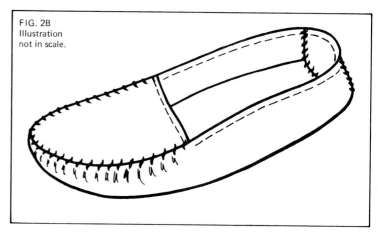

FIG. 2B
Illustration
not in scale.

Patchwork belt

Figure 3 shows how we used up scraps of suede left over from the waistcoat to make a patchwork belt. This is the sort of belt you can make according to your personal taste, so length or width hasn't been indicated.

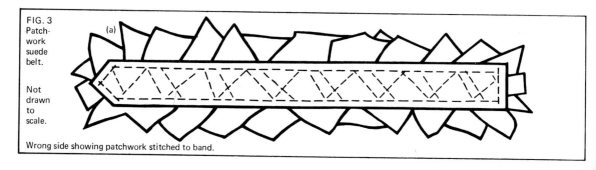

FIG. 3
Patch-
work
suede
belt.

Not
drawn
to
scale.

(a)

Wrong side showing patchwork stitched to band.

First, cut out a band to the length and shape of the finished belt in sailcloth. Then, without attempting to cut the scraps of suede into any particular shape, stitch them to the band, using a wide zigzag stitch on the sewing machine to cover all raw edges. Only when this stitching is completed should you trim all the surplus waste material from round the edges. *3a* shows how the belt looked before it was trimmed.

The next step was to bind the edges with satin bias binding, for a neat finish. Finally, before stitching on the buckle and making eyelet holes at the pointed end, we stitched on coloured suede scraps to brighten up the belt.

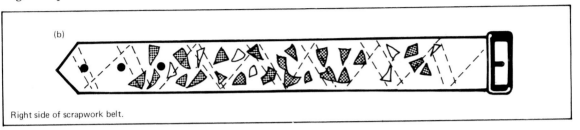

Right side of scrapwork belt.

Belt from circular scraps

Figure 4 shows another type of belt made from leftover scraps. In this case, the pieces were cut evenly into equal-sized circles. For firmness and strength, each circle was backed with a circle of sailcloth stuck on with Copydex. The circles were then overlapped, each one being joined to its neighbour by a small, decorative rivet. To fasten a belt of this kind you can use a chain length or a narrow strap of leather to tone with the circles.

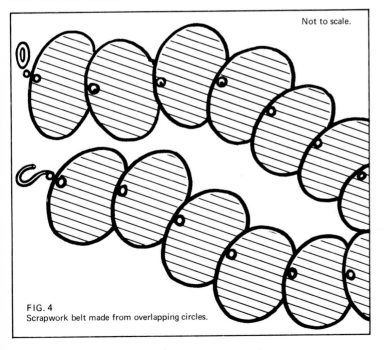

FIG. 4
Scrapwork belt made from overlapping circles.

7 Toymaking

There is nothing more enjoyable and satisfactory than being able to weave a little magic with assorted scraps of material, to produce a toy for a child. And, of course, the best and easiest sort of toy to make is an animal. As you know, a toy animal doesn't have to be perfectly proportioned or the right colour, to be appreciated. In fact, all that is necessary is that he should be recognisable as a member of a particular species.

CHOOSING DESIGNS

The most important consideration when choosing a design for a toy which is to be made in leather is the nature of the material you are going to use. It is not soft and pliable like cloth, and so it cannot be stitched on the inside and turned right side out in the same way. For that reason, it is always easier to plan your work with a view to having most, if not all, your joins on the outside.

Most patterns designed for toys in felt can be used also for the soft leathers which are the only ones really suitable for toy animals. Our patterns are drawn to a scale in which each square represents 1in. However, it is quite easy to alter the size of a pattern, so that the toy is half the size of ours – or even twice as big if you so wish – by the simple expedient of making each square equal to $\frac{1}{2}$in or 2in respectively.

Avoid designs which have long narrow points (ears and a tail, for instance) which are difficult to fill out when it comes to stuffing the toy. And remember that, at every stage of construction, the cut-out animal is going to need special handling because you are working with leather. So don't make the mistake of stitching up the entire outline before inserting the stuffing, even if the pattern designers say this is the correct way of doing things: even though you can use a pattern meant for felt or some other material, the recommended steps may not be in the right order when your material is leather.

Sewing and stuffing

Sewing and stuffing are two steps which go together for, in working with most animal designs, your work will be much easier if you adopt a stuff-as-you-sew routine. In this way, you can fill out such details as tail and ears cut in one with the main material when stitching in that area has been completed, while such details are easily accessible.

As explained earlier, it is difficult to make joinings on the wrong side, unless the design of the animal is very large, so that the work can be turned out easily. It is best, therefore, to work with the right side of the leather out and to make joinings which are going to show and which can even be part of the decoration.

You can, of course, machine-stitch the pieces together. When you do this, you will need to use clothes pegs to hold matching pieces in place, to avoid stretching and unevenness. Follow the directions given for seaming leather in Chapter 6, and use a long stitch and a sharp needle. In this case, seams cannot be trimmed or flattened, so the stitching should be even all round and not more than $\frac{1}{4}$in from the edge. This is a good method to use when you are dealing with a simple outline which allows for continuous stitching. It is not so satisfactory when the design requires the filling-out of details as you go along, since it is not a good idea to keep on interrupting and rejoining stitches.

Another point to bear in mind is the risk that the leather may tear where stitches have been inserted, if the animal is stuffed too tightly. Because of its nature, leather tends to be weakened by stitching; and so if there is too much stuffing the toy may tear easily when the child plays with it, or even if it is handled roughly.

For many types of toys, thonging, using the oversewing method, is easiest. It not only allows you to proceed more slowly, stuffing out the various details as you go along, but it also makes it possible to work with a leather that is lined, and therefore strengthened, in the areas to be stitched. A light, flexible skiver lining can be stuck to a soft leather without affecting the general suppleness of the material.

Decorating

It is best to complete all decorative details before lining or punching the leather. When it's a question of toy-making, you can really get down to experimenting with many of the decorative effects described earlier. Although the type of leather you are using is not suitable for tooling or modelling, it is ideal for painting, dyeing and appliqué work of all kinds. For example, you could have features such as eyes, nose, or a mouth, that are painted on or stitched on. And even if the finished animal looks rather like a caricature of the real thing, this only adds to the fun.

For details such as eyes and spots, work with the material flat on the table. Cut each piece out carefully and use a rubber-based adhesive to stick it in place. The adhesive may be sufficiently strong on its own, but if the spot is a large one, it is best to use a long straight stitch, or a large zigzag stitch to outline it.

Do remember also that the animal has two sides, each of which are equally important. Any detail at points which are adjoining should be correctly matched, but others – such as spots – can be distributed more freely.

The question of gussets

For a quite satisfactory toy animal, all you need are two identically cut pieces of leather joined together in the simple manner we have been describing.

However, if you want to make an animal that can be placed in a standing position, then you will need to introduce a further dimension, and this is achieved by means of a gusset inserted between the two shaped pieces.

Whether used in dressmaking or in the construction of a bag or an animal, a gusset serves the same purpose: it gives shape and an increased capacity. However, gussets need very careful fitting and, when it comes to toy-making, this can be difficult even when you are working with soft, cloth fabrics. For this reason, they are best avoided except when dealing with plain and straightforward shapes in which you can use two simple body outlines and a straight gusset.

If you do decide to use a gusset, however, you can still use the same type of pattern as we have been describing. The only extra material you need is a strip long enough to go round the animal's outline. The

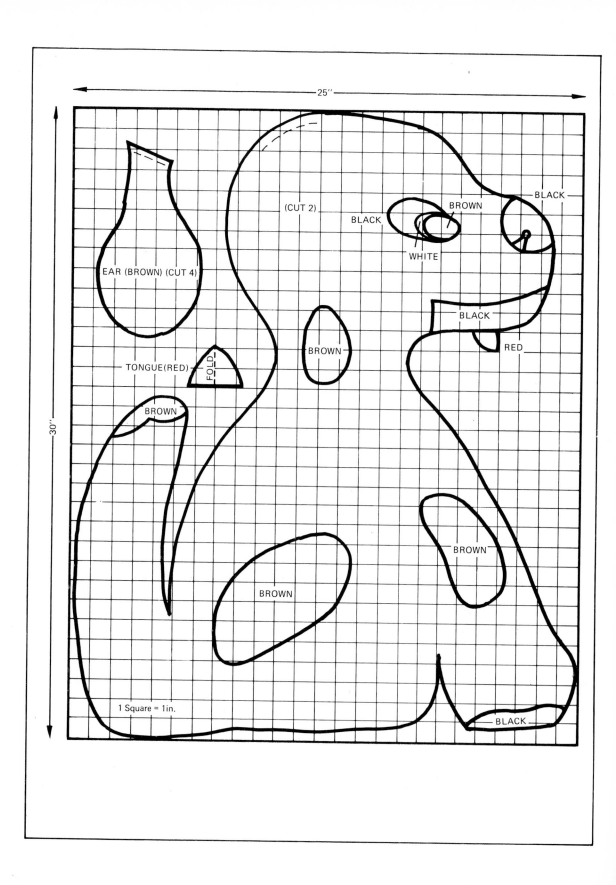

25"

30"

(CUT 2)

BLACK

BROWN

BLACK

WHITE

EAR (BROWN) (CUT 4)

BLACK

RED

TONGUE(RED)

FOLD

BROWN

BROWN

BROWN

BROWN

BROWN

1 Square = 1in.

BLACK

width of the strip is optional, but 2in or 3in should be enough for a small toy. You can then have a slight narrowing of the strip (which should be equal on both sides) to give additional shaping at the neck, for instance.

The most important thing about fitting a gusset is that the fit must be perfectly matched on both sides of the animal. This is a matter for very careful measuring and marking, following the steps described for the marking of bag gussets in Chapter 2.

In other respects, the toy is completed in the same way as if the joining involved only two layers of material.

Toy dog

We have made this dog in white basil, and used scraps of brown and black leather for spots and features.

Requirements

2 pieces of leather, each measuring 30in by 25in; 2 pieces of skiver lining to match above measurements; plastic foam or other suitable stuffing; thonging and $\frac{1}{2}$yd of chain to make necklet; scraps of leather or suede in different colours.

To make dog

When cutting out, be careful to turn pattern over when cutting out second side, otherwise you may have two sides which are identical and won't match.

Cut out and attach pieces to represent features and spots, as explained in Chapter 7. Punch round outline.

Use paper clips or clothes pegs to hold matching edges together while thonging. Start at the lower edge where the most difficult detail – the tail – can be completed and filled out at an early stage in the work.

When you reach the face, fold the triangular piece for the tongue in two and stick the layers together. Then catch it in with the thonging which joins the mouth edges.

Make the ears and attach these to the head in the same way. The length of chain joined to encircle the neck completes the dog.

List of suppliers of leather and tools

Rose Fittings, 337 City Road, London WC1.
Prime Leathers Limited, Tottenham Street, London W1.
Light Leather Company Limited, 18 Newman Street, London W1.
Honeywill Limited, 22a Fouberts Place, London W1.
Northern Handicrafts Limited, Bellvue Mill, Westgate, Burnley B. B11 15D.
S. Glassner, 68 Worple Road, Wimbledon, London SW19.

The first three firms on the list supply leather only. Northern Handicrafts will supply a catalogue on request. However, you should be able to buy many of the tools, trims and fittings you need in the haberdashery or handicraft department of most large stores. You will find many items made up in handy packs and at reasonable prices.
American readers should be able to find leather wholesalers in Gloversville, New York, such as Cayadutta Tanning and Eton Leathers.